# Grounded Faith for Growing Christians

### By Sam E. Stone

Obtain a 40-page leader's guide to accompany this paperback. Order number 1957 from Standard Publishing or your local supplier.

A Division of Standard Publishing
Cincinnati, Ohio 45231
No. 2293

P9-APO-494

Chapter themes based on International Bible Lessons for Christian Teaching, © 1971 by the Lesson Committee.
 © 1975, The STANDARD PUBLISHING Company.

Library of Congress Catalog No. 74-79116
ISBN 0-87239-006-3

Printed in U.S.A.                                        1975

# Table of Contents

# DEDICATION

to my wife, Gwen,
who helps my Christian
growth more than anyone.

# INTRODUCTION

Every swimmer can find a challenge in the ocean. The beginner can wade at the water's edge; the learner can find excitement and adventure farther out; yet even the most experienced swimmer cannot touch bottom in the deepest parts.

The Bible is like that.

Every growing Christian can find challenge and guidance from God's Word. The interested inquirer may start at the "edge," simply meeting Jesus in the Gospels. The believer may find stimulation and satisfaction in intensive study both of the Old and New Testaments. But the depths of wisdom in Scripture can never be plumbed by even the most enlightened. Always there is something new to learn!

This book can help you grow as a Christian. Section one suggests our chief resource for growth—the Bible. Section two offers practical guidance in the real-life situations which develop mature faith.

Hopefully you'll agree, "It is more blessed to grow than to recede."

# 1

# TELL IT
# LIKE IT IS

Imagine yourself on a lonely road late at night. Your car breaks down. You need help. Then you see a telephone booth nearby. To receive help, you need just one thing—a coin.

No houses are nearby. No traffic. You search your pockets. There are some bills, some credit cards. But you need that coin! It is your only hope.

For millions stranded on the lonely road of despair today, there is also just one hope—the Bible. God's Word is the bread of life which alone can satisfy spiritual hunger.

The Bible demands attention. It has endured for centuries. It has been translated into over 200 languages and parts of it into over 1100 tongues. It is the world's all-time best seller.

This book can't be just another book any more than Christianity can be just another religion. It is no take-it-or-leave-it offer. If the Bible is true, all eternity hinges on your response to it. This book tells it like it is.

God commanded men to write His message. Jesus

spoke. But the only way that we can know what He said for sure is because Matthew, Mark, Luke, and John wrote it down. Oral reports change, but not the written word. We have in Scripture a permanent, accurate account. Readers can ponder new truth and study it again. It provides a guidebook for Christian growth.

Through the ages, God's Word has met with varied responses. The devil questioned it. Eve tested it. She and Adam disobeyed it. Noah endured ridicule because of it. Abraham left his home on account of it. The psalmist found it sweeter than honey. Prophets were persecuted for preaching it. Kings tried to destroy it. But, through the centuries, the truly wise and happy have believed and obeyed it!

## Record

Obedient servants recorded the divine message in written form. They gave us what we need to know. You can almost see John shake his head in wonder as he exclaims, "But there are also many other things which Jesus did; were every one of them to be written, I suppose that the world itself could not contain the books that would be written" (John 21:25 RSV).

God chose to reveal himself to man in progressive stages. This gradual unfolding in Bible history has been described as the starlight, moonlight, and finally the sunlight age.

When you drive down the interstate, you may see a white car parked ahead on the shoulder of the road. As you get closer, you notice a small black instrument protruding from the driver's window. When you pass the car, you note the "state highway patrol" emblem on the door. *Then* you check your speedometer!

You didn't learn all those facts at once. Had the uniformed officer wanted to tell you he was there, he might have posted a sign a few miles back saying, "radar unit ahead." He could have had his red light flashing and his siren blaring. But that was not his purpose.

In a similar gradual way, though for a different reason, God chose to disclose himself to man. He did this at various times in differing ways. God revealed himself to the world through *creation* (Romans 1:19). He again revealed himself through *incarnation* (as Jesus was born). Then in the Bible, He manifested himself in *revelation.* In the first He revealed His power; in the second, His love; and in the third, His will. That's how we got the Bible.

Kenneth Taylor paraphrases Hebrews 1:1 like this: "Long ago God spoke in many different ways to our fathers through the prophets [in visions, dreams, and even face to face], telling them little by little about his plans."

God told Eve that through her seed the serpent's head would be crushed.

God told Abraham that through him all nations of the earth would be blessed.

God told Judah that Shiloh would come before the scepter departed from Him.

God told the Israelites that He would raise up a prophet like Moses whom they should follow.

God told the psalmist of the suffering Messiah and the resurrected Lord.

To Moses, He spoke in storm and thunder; to Elijah, in a still, small voice. But God has now spoken with finality in His Son. The New Testament of Jesus Christ is His final revelation.

## Receive

The Lord commands us to listen. When you read the Bible, you can hear God talking. It's that simple. Charles Schulz, the creator of Peanuts, also draws clever cartoons about Christian teenagers. In one he shows a high school boy telling his girlfriend, "I think I've finally begun to unravel the mystery of the Old Testament. I've started to read it."

The boy is right! Get a Bible. Start to read it. If you get hung up on the Shakespearean English of the King James Version, try one of the modern speech translations. But read it! There's no better way to understand it.

There's something in it for you. When God told Jeremiah to write, He explained:

Take a scroll and write on it all the words that I have spoken to you against Israel and Judah and all the nations, ... It may be that the house of Judah will hear all the evil which I intend to do to them, so that every one may turn from his evil way, and that I may forgive their iniquity and their sin (Jeremiah 36:2, 3 RSV).

We need to hear like they heard. If we'd read the Bible with the diligence and interest we give to a newspaper, that would help. We put each news article in the context of present events in order to understand it. While the Bible differs from other books in that it is divinely inspired, the same basic rules of interpretation apply to it also. We still need logic and common sense if we want to know the author's meaning. Here are three practical guidelines:

1. When you read a passage, ask yourself first who is speaking.

2. Discover to whom the author is writing.

3. Then determine the setting and circumstances.

Properly interpreted, Scripture does not contradict itself. Use good judgment as you seek the meaning of a text. Compare various translations to help. The Bible is its own best commentary.

A student at The Cincinnati Bible Seminary once asked Professor R. C. Foster, "Should a person interpret the Bible literally or figuratively?"

He quickly responded, "Neither—but intelligently!"

God commands us to receive His Word. We should normally take a passage as literal unless the context clearly requires that it be considered figurative. Our main need is to desire to know and understand the message.

A Bible-school teacher was trying to help her class visualize the time when Moses gave the Israelites water in the wilderness. She asked, "What do you think of when you're real thirsty?"

Little Dale thought a moment. Then he piped up, "Kool Aid!"

We don't always thirst for the right things. We must want to hear God's Word.

## Respond

But hearing God's Word alone is insufficient.

We must respond to it.

Some scholars tell us that in our enlightened age, this book is out of date. But these self-appointed critics can make mistakes. They may be like the absent-minded professor who came home late one night, put his cigar in bed, and threw himself out the window. Multitudes are holding on to the charred stub of materialism while they toss their eternal destiny out the window of neglect.

When Moses announced God's laws to the people, they answered, "We will obey them all" (Exodus 24:3 LB). Then he wrote them down. He read them aloud again. And again the people said, "We solemnly promise to obey every one of these rules" (Exodus 24:7 LB). Forty days and eight chapters later, we read the untimely end of their noble resolution!

Talking about obedience isn't enough. Hearing the Bible and merely saying we believe it do not satisfy the Lord. Jesus warned, "Not every one who says to me, 'Lord, Lord,' shall enter the kingdom of heaven, but he who does the will of my Father who is in Heaven" (Matthew 7:21 RSV).

Use the following checklist of questions to help learn and obey what the Bible says. When you read a chapter, ask yourself:

● What is the main point or lesson in this chapter?
● Does it apply to me and have I learned it?

- What promise can I claim?
- What command do I need to obey or what example do I need to follow?
- What warning do I need to hear?
- What verse do I have difficulty in understanding or applying? (Talk to a minister, elder, or Bible-school teacher for help.)
- What is new for me to learn about my God and Savior? What old truth is shown here in a new light?
- What thought in this chapter do I want to share with someone? Who?
- What verse will I memorize from it? (Write it out and learn it.)

Ross H. Dampier tells about a great preacher of the early 1900's, John Shepherd. He preached Jesus wherever he could. After one evening service, he felt uneasy about setting out on a mountain trail. The night was dark and stormy.

His host went to the fireplace and took a branch that had on its end a blazing pine knot. "Take it," said the mountaineer. "It will light you home."

Brother Shepherd told of the event in a sermon some months later. "So I took it," he said, "and it lit me home." Then he lifted high his worn Bible and said to his hearers, "Take it, my friends, it will light you home."

## Grounded Faith for Growing Christians

Now that you've read this chapter, try these Scripture passages: Exodus 24:3-8; Jeremiah 36:1-4; Revelation 1:10, 11.

# 2

# HEAR THE WORD OF THE LORD

A capable Christian repairman had been called to service the mechanism in a giant telescope. During his lunch hour, he was reading the New Testament while he ate. The chief astronomer saw him and smiled. "What good do you expect to get out of that? With our scientific achievements, the Bible is completely outdated. Why you can't even be sure who wrote it!"

The mechanic was silent a moment. Then he looked up. "Don't you use the multiplication tables quite a bit in your calculations?"

"Why, certainly," the astronomer replied.

"Do you know who wrote them?" the Christian asked.

"No, I guess I don't," he admitted.

"Then how can you use them when you aren't sure of the author?"

"We trust them because—well—because they work," finished the scientist with a note of irritation.

"Well," said the Christian, "I trust the Bible for the same reason."

While many strong evidences confirm the fact that the

Bible is God's Word, the Christian also has his personal experience to help verify his faith. Consider the nature of the Bible.

## Different

The Bible is a lot like other books.

You can read it just as you would a paperback from the drugstore.

You find nothing magical about the paper on which it's printed.

You need not lay aside logic, reason, and clear thinking before you start to read.

The Bible *is* a lot like other books.

*But the Bible is different.*

It has a supernatural source. Despite men's worst efforts to stamp it out, this volume has met the test of time and culture. It proves itself anew to every generation, every race, every nation, every need.

An "underground" high school club in a Midwest city prided itself in flaunting traditions and custom. A Christian boy was being inducted one night. They met in an old garage.

When he went inside, he found the other fellows lining the wall. A trash barrel was at the other end with a fire going in it. One of the boys handed him a Bible. "Your initiation is to go throw this in there," he told the Christian.

The boy hesitated. Someone snickered. Another sneered. He started toward the container, held the Bible over the fire, and then suddenly drew it back. He said, "Fellows, let's don't throw this book away until we're sure we've got a better one to take its place."

William Lyon Phelps, professor at Yale University, declared, "I thoroughly believe in a university education for both men and women; but I believe a knowledge of the Bible without a college course is more valuable than a college course without the Bible."

## Defensible

Some doubt the Bible.

Don't let that worry you. The Christian doesn't need to run and hide when he meets skeptics. He has nothing to fear. The Bible is true—and all truth is mutually consistent. When properly interpreted, Scripture harmonizes with all truth in any other field. The more one learns of the Bible, the more convinced he becomes that it is the Word of the Lord. Jesus helped honest doubters (like Thomas)—and so must we!

Fulfilled prophecy is one of the strongest evidences for the Scripture's validity. The life and teaching of Jesus also set an unsurpassed standard. Christ's resurrection is one of the best attested facts of history. The Christian may rest on these facts as he defends his faith in the arena of current thought. (You will find valuable resources in Paul Little's helpful book, *Know Why You Believe,* published by Inter-Varsity Press.)

If the Bible is God's Word, it can stand the test of honest inquiry. Never fear to study. When questions arise, find Bible-believing scholars who can help clear them up. Be fair enough to hear both sides—not just the caustic criticism of an agnostic professor.

Perhaps the charge that does most to undermine faith in Scripture is the allegation that the Bible contradicts itself. If the Bible contains statements contrary to known truth, or if it has mistakes, it may not be considered an accurate account (at least in that place and to that extent).

When someone tells you that contradictions exist in the Bible, ask him for some examples. Frequently the doubter is simply parroting what he has heard another say—without ever doing any firsthand investigation. This is far from being intellectually honest!

A young minister's wife was enrolled in a California state college. One professor seemed to delight in running down God, the Bible, and Christians in particular.

One afternoon he proclaimed, "I don't know how anyone can believe the Bible. Everyone knows there are so many hopeless contradictions in it."

Barbara raised her hand. "Professor, could you give us some examples of them?"

The professor's face turned red. He walked over to her desk. He stood in silence a moment. Then he exploded.

"What are you trying to do—make me admit that I don't know what I'm talking about!"

*And he couldn't name a one!*

This is the point. It is one thing to make a sweeping generalization; it is another to have the facts of honest study to back it up.

Study any alleged contradictions in the light of the guidelines given in chapter one (page 11). Any reconcilable difference is not a contradiction. If passages treat different subjects, or use one word in two different senses, they are not contradictory. Unless one affirms what another denies, there is no contradiction. Different events may resemble each other. (When passages seem to conflict, one should take the definite and specific as the standard.)

Seth Wilson reminds us, "One need only prove that his hypothetical explanation of the alleged contradiction is possible (that conditions existed to permit it). When this has been done, the accounts are sufficiently defended."

## Divine

The Bible is a divine book. Written by some forty men, in several countries, over some 1500 years, the majestic unity of this "library" is astounding. It is indeed "The Book."

Peter stressed this unique quality of Scripture when he wrote:

For we did not follow cleverly devised myths when we made known to you the power and coming of our Lord Jesus Christ, but we were eyewitnesses of his majesty, . . . because no prophecy ever came by the impulse of man, but men moved by the Holy Spirit spoke from God (2 Peter 1:16, 21 RSV).

The Bible is not just another book.

This book is special.

Luke explained this in the preface to his Gospel:

Several biographies of Christ have already been written using as their source material the reports circulating among us from the early disciples and other eyewitnesses. However, it occurred to me that it would be well to recheck all these accounts from first to last and after thorough investigation to pass this summary on to you, to reassure you of the truth of all you were taught (Luke 1:1-4 LB).

Biblical writers wanted to convince their readers. Merely telling someone doesn't always get the message across though. It can turn out as it did for a temperance lecturer. Speaking to a children's group, he arranged an impressive demonstration. He had two beakers—one filled with alcohol, one with water. He dropped an earthworm into the water. The worm wiggled around and the speaker took him out.

Next he dropped the worm into the alcohol. The worm died. "Now, boys and girls," said the speaker triumphantly, "what does this teach you?"

One little girl put up her hand. "It means if you drink alcohol, you won't have worms!"

That wasn't quite the message he intended to convey!

People may misunderstand. This is one reason that God used the changeless written Word as our source for Christian faith and growth. He confirmed the apostolic message by miraculous sign. Through the ages, this record has been preserved for us.

John Wesley put it like this: "I am a creature of a day. I am a spirit come from God and returning to God. I want to know one thing: the way to heaven. God himself has condescended to teach me the way. He has written it down in a book. O give me that book! At any price give me the book of God! Let me be a man of one book".

## Definitive

It serves as an objective standard by which we can measure our doctrine and life.

Our Roman Catholic friends disagree. They insist that since the church gave the world the Bible, the church has the right to change or modify the Bible. Their logic quickly breaks down. True, the New Testament did not exist as such during the first century of Christianity—but God's Word was already at work. It was God's Word which called the church into being (see Romans 10:14-17; Acts 2). The *written* word is a record of the *spoken* word of God. Therefore no man or group of men has authority to change this divine volume. It is definitive in all matters of faith. We are accountable to it.

"So while the evangelical Christian emphasizes a personal knowledge of God through Christ, he insists that God has also revealed himself in the words of Scripture," declares Dr. Daniel P. Fuller. He adds, "Scripture must ever be the control for our personal knowledge of God, and the only infallible rule of faith and practice."

In his helpful volume *Understanding the Bible* (published by Regal Books), John R. W. Stott declares:

> If Jesus Christ is truly our teacher and our lord, we are under both His instruction and His authority. We must therefore bring our mind into subjection to Him as our teacher and our will into subjection to Him as our Lord. We have no liberty to disagree with Him or to disobey Him. So we bow to the authority of Scripture because we bow to the authority of Christ" (p. 203).

## Demanding

George was asked, "What do you believe?"

He answered, "I believe what my church believes."

The querist pressed further. "Then what does your church believe?"

"It believes what I believe," he replied.

Finally his friend said, "And what do you *both* believe?"

"George smiled. "Why, we both believe the same thing!"

This isn't good enough. God directs us, "Always be prepared to make a defense to any one who calls you to account for the hope that is in you, yet do it with gentleness and reverence" (1 Peter 3:15 RSV). Claiming the Bible as a rule of faith and practice cannot be used to escape personal responsibility in study, interpretation, and application.

We need to know the Bible. In Old Testament times, the Lord directed that His commandments be taught thoroughly to the Hebrew people (Deuteronomy 6:1-9).

Paul told Timothy that Scripture was valuable for teaching, reproof, correction, and training in right living (2 Timothy 3:14-17). Because the Bible is God's book, it instructs men about salvation. A special blessing is promised the one who reads it (Revelation 1:3).

The Bible offers man the truth of God and the hope of Christ. It brings psalms of comfort, proverbs of guidance, lessons of history, and four Gospels which give the one best book at the singular life of Jesus. It alone answers man's question, "What must I do to be saved?" It is indeed the Word of the Lord!

## Grounded Faith for Growing Christians

Now that you've read this chapter, try these Scripture passages: Deuteronomy 6:1-9; Luke 1:1-4; 2 Timothy 3:14-17; 2 Peter 1:20, 21.

# 3

# WHY WAS THE BIBLE WRITTEN?

A baboon sat in a zoo cage with a Bible in one hand and an evolution textbook in the other. He reportedly explained, "I'm trying to find out if I am my brother's keeper or my keeper's brother!"

The Bible can settle questions like that.

This is one reason God gave us Scripture—to let us learn things we could find out in no other way.

Unless one accepts the Bible as God's Word, he is forced to Plato's conclusion. The Greek philosopher said that one must "take the best and most irrefragable of human theories, and let this be the raft upon which he sails through life—not without risk, unless he can find some word of God which will more surely and safely carry him" (*Phaedo,* 85b).

We are not left to drift on a sea of confusion, however. The Bible claims to be a divine revelation. It has been attested as such. John put it like this:

That which was from the beginning, which we have heard, which we have seen with our eyes, which we have looked upon and touched with our hands, concerning the word of life—the life was made manifest, and we saw it, and testify to it, and proclaim to you the eternal life which was with the Father and was made manifest to us—that which we have seen and heard we proclaim also to you, so that you may have fellowship with us; and our fellowship is with the Father and with his Son Jesus Christ. And we are writing this that our joy may be complete (1 John 1:1-4 RSV).

This suggests some of the reasons why the Bible was written.

## Faith

"I've been there. I'm telling it like it is." So we might paraphrase John's confident testimony of his personal acquaintance with God's Son. Three or more years of intimate fellowship, day in and day out, made the apostle an unimpeachable witness to Christ's resurrection.

He declares in his Gospel:

Now Jesus did many other signs in the presence of the disciples, which are not written in this book; but these are written that you may believe that Jesus is the Christ, the Son of God, and that believing you may have life in his name (John 20:30, 31 RSV).

The basic purpose of the Gospels was to produce faith in Christ as God's Son. Luke wrote so that his readers might know the certainty concerning the things they had been taught (Luke 1:4). Apostolic journalism had an evangelistic purpose.

Other New Testament books were designed to engender hope, answer personal challenges, reply to questions from the churches, correct heresies, and show the relative importance of various Christian teachings.

We need an objective source of faith which the Bible provides.

A father had his little girl with him at the lake. She wanted to row the boat. He explained that she should pick an object directly opposite the place she wanted to reach. "Keep your eye on it, and you'll go straight across."

But they didn't! Their course was zigzagged. Finally her father asked, "What object are you looking at?"

"That red boat," pointed the girl.

In life as in boating, a moving object makes a straight course difficult to follow. Those who adopt the "new morality" find it conflicts with the changeless Biblical norm. Others try to fit in with whatever crowd they're with. They soon learn that a true Christian can't be a chameleon.

To have certainty and purpose, one must follow a true guide. The Bible fits that description. You can put your faith in it. The God of the Bible is the all-powerful Creator and Sustainer of the universe.

When my son, Jeff, was four years old, we were riding in the car one afternoon. He asked me to tell him a Bible story. I picked David and Goliath. "The Philistines were trying to conquer the Israelites," I began.

"What's 'conquer'?" he interrupted.

"That means they were trying to take over God's people and capture them," I explained.

He laughed and said, "They wouldn't get away with that with God around!"

That's faith. Faith in the God of the Bible. He can take care of us. This is one lesson the holy writings teach. Scripture was also written so that we might have fellowship.

## Fellowship

Originally man had fellowship with God. The Lord walked with man in the garden. Sin broke the companionship. Nothing man could do would restore it. It remained for God in His infinite love to provide the means by which fellowship could be restored—He gave Jesus to save us.

From childhood Timothy was taught "the sacred writings which are able to instruct you for salvation through faith in Christ Jesus" (2 Timothy 3:15 RSV). Even the Old

Testament writings could lead one to the Savior, Paul explains. Salvation comes as we use knowledge gained from Scripture to put our faith in Jesus. Through obedience to Him, we can have fellowship with God again.

Simply reading the Bible or hearing God's Word does not of itself insure salvation, of course. Jeremiah received this divine directive:

> Stand out in front of the Temple of the Lord and make an announcement to all the people who have come there to worship from many parts of Judah. Give them the entire message; don't leave out one word of all I have for them to hear. For perhaps they will listen and turn from their evil ways, and then I can withhold all the punishment I am ready to pour out upon them because of their evil deeds (Jeremiah 26:2, 3 LB).

Because the Bible is of such great import, we must *make* time for regular, daily study of it. A Chinese Christian made this rule, "No Bible, no breakfast." He would not eat food in the morning until he had first found spiritual food, the bread of life.

Billy Graham has this Bible reading plan: he reads five chapters of Psalms each day and one chapter of Proverbs. By this method, he reads both books once each month (in addition to other Bible reading). He said, "Proverbs keeps me right with man and Psalms keeps me right with God."

Whatever method of Bible reading you choose, stick to it. See the need for daily fellowship with God. Times of prayer let you talk to God; but reading the Word lets Him speak to you.

## Fulfillment

Fulfillment also comes when one reads the Bible. Jesus assured us, "I came that they might have life, and might have it abundantly" (John 10:10 NAS). John wrote that our joy might be complete (1 John 1:4).

Read the account of Jesus' walk with the two going to Emmaus (Luke 24:13-35). Imagine the thrill they felt as the risen Lord answered all of their questions about "Jesus of Nazareth, who was a prophet mighty in deed and word before God and all the people" (Luke 24:19 RSV).

Christ began with Moses. Then He spoke of the prophets. He outlined for them the predictions of His life, death, and resurrection that thread the Old Testament. Describing the event later, the two exclaimed, "Did not our hearts burn within us, . . . while he opened to us the scriptures?" (verse 32). Not only is Jesus the fulfillment of the hundreds of prophecies made about Him, He also provides the personal fulfillment and satisfaction each man needs.

Pascal called it "a God-shaped vacuum" in the heart of each man. Augustine put it like this, "Thou madest us for Thyself, and our heart is restless, until it repose in Thee." Only God satisfies.

A Stone Age Indian in Central America heard the Bible for the first time in his own language. When he did, he exclaimed, "Ah, that book—it speaks to my stomach!"

That's why the Bible was written. It "puts it all together." It gives meaning and purpose to life. It meets our needs; it answers our questions; it stands like the towering Himalayas over all the writings of men.

God gave us the Bible because we had to have it. The owner's manual of a car contains the maker's instructions for proper use to achieve maximum success. In a similar way, the Bible is the Owner's manual for man. God made us. He has given us these guidelines which, if followed, bring pleasure, success, and satisfaction.

Lynn Gardner suggests an interesting situation. "What if a lone astronaut streaking through outer space in a rocket ship accidentally were to strike his head on some object, causing him to have amnesia? When he regains consciousness he can still think and talk, but he cannot remember any of his training as a space man. He does not know where he is or why. His only chance of survival is to obey exactly the messages communicated to him from the space scientists in Houston, Texas. His salvation would depend on their accurate information on how to return to earth."

Man in the world finds himself in a similar predicament. We do not know who we are nor why we are in the world unless the One who made us and put us here tells us. We cannot save ourselves. We can recognize the guilt in our hearts but we cannot free ourselves from it. We do not know how best to live this life, nor if there is a life after death, unless God tells us.

For faith, for fellowship, for fulfillment—that's why the Bible was written!

## Grounded Faith for Growing Christians

Now that you've read this chapter, try these Scripture passages: Jeremiah 26:1-3; Luke 24:13-47; John 20:30, 31; 1 John 1:1-4.

# 4

# HOW
# THE BIBLE
# HELPS US

An old fable tells how a lad received a magic key from a genie. It would unlock every room in a vast storehouse of treasures. "Take all you want in any room," the genie warned the boy, "but don't forget the very best."

The boy filled his arms with gold nuggets, picked up the key, and went home. The next day he carried out an armful of silver bars, then beautiful rubies on the next. On the following day, he returned.

*This is wonderful,* he thought. *I'm rich. I'll always have all I need.* He unlocked a door which opened into a room of glittering diamonds. Laying down the key, he grabbed all of the precious stones he could carry and hurried out. As the door closed behind him, the genie appeared.

With horror the boy realized he had left the key inside. "Let me back in," he begged.

The genie shook his head. "I cannot do that. Remember how I warned you—take all you want, but don't forget the very best."

This applies to the Bible. Take all of the good in life, but don't forget what is the very best. God's Word alone holds the key to a happy eternity!

It is not, however, just a word of inspiration to be opened at random with a perfect message for every specific situation.

One man who felt this way had a rather sad experience. He was searching for a verse to cheer him up. He just let the Bible fall open. Eyes closed, he pointed to a text. It read: "And Judas went out and hanged himself." That wasn't too consoling, so he decided to try again.

Again he let the Bible fall open, closed his eyes, and pointed to a text. "Go thou and do likewise." That really frustrated him, so he tried once more. This time he read, "What thou doest, do quickly."

It's dangerous to use the Bible like this!

Neither is the Bible a magic charm. Vonda Kay Van Dyke was asked in the Miss America Pageant if she viewed the Bible as a good luck symbol. She replied in essence, "I do not. To me it is a guide book for life."

The Bible can't help you if you don't use it. Our fathers used to quote David's words with meaning: "Thy word have I hid in mine heart, that I might not sin against thee" (Psalm 119:11 KJV). Today many seem content to stop with the first five words: "Thy word have I hid!" Under the *T.V. Guide,* the sports magazine, and the *Reader's Digest,* The Bible lies on a table. Like medicine, it doesn't help unless we use it. But when we do, the Bible aids us in many ways.

## Instruction (Romans 15:4)

Scripture instructs us. "For whatever was written in earlier times was written for our instruction, that through perseverance and the encouragement of the Scriptures we might have hope" (Romans 15:4 NAS).

It reaches from another sphere of life and shows us divine truth. Isaiah explains that God's thoughts are not ours. His ways are above and beyond our ways (Isaiah 55:8-11).

The Bible shows the perspective of history. History repeats itself because men fail to learn from it. If you wish to know how to live today, the Bible is more up-to-date than tomorrow's newspaper.

A college girl discovered an amazing similarity when she studied the Old Testament. "Fellows today are just like Samson," she explained. "They're impulsive, brag about their strength, and wear their hair too long!"

## Correction (Psalm 19)

The Bible also provides correction. The psalmist asked, "Who can discern his errors?" In that same song of praise to God's Word, he answered his question: "The commandment of the Lord is pure, enlightening the eyes, . . . Moreover by them is thy servant warned; in keeping them there is great reward" (Psalm 19:8, 11 RSV).

This book will keep you from sin—or sin will keep you from this book. Study of the Bible shows us our wrongdoing. Sermons may make us uncomfortable. The way to feel better is not to quit listening to sermons, but to change our lives!

Speaking of Psalm 19:6, C. S. Lewis says, "As the psalmist felt the sun in the desert searching him out in every nook of shade, so he feels the law searching the hiding-places of his soul" *(Reflections on the Psalms,* Geoffrey Bles Ltd., London; p. 64). That's what the Bible does.

In *Pilgrim's Progress,* Christian is asked by Mr. Worldly Wiseman how he came to have the heavy burden (of sin) upon his back. "By reading this Book in my hand," Christian replied.

"I thought so," said Worldly. He then tried to direct him to the Village of Morality and get him to leave the Book alone. But Christian found no relief. Only when he came to the cross of Jesus did the burden fall from his back.

You need the Bible. The baseball player or fan may differ with the umpire's call. In the same way we may disagree with others who judge us, but we can't disagree with God. We must hear Him. We need His correction if we are to reach heaven. John Newton sang:

May the gospel's joyful sound
Conquer sinners, comfort saints,
Make the fruits of grace abound,
Bring relief to all complaints;
Thus may all our worship prove,
Till we join the church above;
Thus may all our worship prove,
Till we join the church above.

## Protection (Psalm 119:7-11, 105, 130)

During the fiery conflict in Viet Nam, the newspapers reported how U.S. Army PFC Roger Boe learned one value of a Bible. While on patrol near Lai Khe, he was ambushed by North Vietnamese soldiers.

When the fighting ended, Boe noticed smoke curling from his pocket. An enemy rifle bullet had gone through his wallet and lodged in his Bible, just short of a loaded ammunition clip. The young soldier said, "That's as close as I want to come."

The Bible offers protection, not just from enemy bullets, but from all of life's perils. You can meet your problems with courage and calm if you remember Romans 8:28. You can keep the right priorities of life if you don't forget Matthew 6:33. You need never sink into despair because of sin and guilt if you cling to John 3:16.

A most practical leaflet is available from the American Bible Society. It tells "where to look in the Bible." Specific Scriptures are cited for times you feel discouraged, lonely, or thankful. If you are getting married, lose your job, or start a new business, it suggests still other passages. (You may write for it at 1865 Broadway, New York, N.Y., 10023).

Herbert J. Taylor, past president of Rotary International, declared: "We eat food to nourish the physical body. Our spiritual body, too . . . requires food and it is my experience that by spending at least one hour daily reading the Bible, it will be nourished."

He adds, "In the Bible I find the answers to my troubles and problems and, I believe, any other devoted reader will have a similar experience."

"Reading the Bible regularly and faithfully can . . . bring to us most of life's greatest treasures—happiness, success, faith, peace of mind, calmness, patience, character, love, friendship, humility, and anticipation of and hope for eternal life."

It's what we need. Someone told of the sympathetic man on a dock who called to a drowning chap, "I can't swim. Would $10 help?" There are times when we can clearly see the emptiness of material things. We need that which has eternal worth. The Bible gives it to us.

## Provision (Matthew 4:1-11)

The Bible gives spiritual life. It gives meaning to life. It gives eternal life. "The words that I have spoken to you are spirit and life" (John 6:63 RSV).

Just as the Word helped Jesus overcome temptation, so it can help us resist Satan. Hiding the Word in our heart—memorizing it—keeps us from sin.

Dwight L. Moody was challenged once to debate an atheist. He agreed, on one condition: the unbeliever must produce on the platform ten or more people who could tell what atheism had done to make them better people. Moody explained that he could have at least a hundred there who could tell how Christ radically changed their lives. From drunkenness, debauchery, and sloth, they had become pure, clean people. Unable to produce the testimonials, the atheist withdrew his offer. It is the gospel that is God's power unto salvation (Romans 1:16, 17).

When you learn this, the Bible becomes what you desire for growth. A Christian missionary, Mel Huckins, told of an experience with lepers on Ryukyu Island.

"Everyone knows," he explained, "that the braille Bible is for those who are sightless. But how can a blind man read when leprosy removes his fingers?"

He told of one devout Christian who used a tender spot on the remaining stub of his hand to read. When his hand was gone, he used his tongue to "read" the braille Bible.

When he continued, his doctor warned that continual reading with his tongue would cause him to lose the ability to taste food. He advised him to quit reading the Bible.

The Christian leper replied, "Food will nourish even if I can't taste it, but if I give up reading the Bible, nothing can nourish my soul." To him, God's Word was truly sweeter than honey (Psalm 19:10). How much does the Word mean to you? How much is it worth?

## Grounded Faith for Growing Christians

Now that you've read this chapter, try these Scripture passages: Psalms 19:7-14; Matthew 4:1-11.

# 5

# HOW CHRISTIAN GROWTH BEGINS

One picture, the ancients say, is worth a thousand words. Our Lord knew this truth. Much of His teaching was in story form for this reason. A parable, an illustration, a picture in words—by this He could clarify the most complex of subjects.

He could have said to His disciples, "Your unity, sustenance and fertility are dependent upon your close proximity to me in all exigencies." Instead He put it in a picture: "I am the vine, you are the branches" (John 15:5 NAS). This says it all.

## Cause

Christian growth begins in the Vine. Branches have unity because of the Vine. The Vine feeds them, allowing them to grow. No branch cut off from the Vine can of itself produce fruit. Jesus, the true Vine, is the cause of Christian growth.

Even the choice of a *vine* to illustrate His point was meaningful. In the Old Testament, Israel had often been pictured as a vine. Jeremiah called it "a right seed"

(2:21). The psalmist spoke of the vine brought out of Egypt (Psalm 80:8). Isaiah, Ezekiel, Joel, Zechariah, and Malachi all used this word picture. It meant something to the Jewish listener.

"As they are not a collection of individuals, but a corporate society, the new Israel of God—it is natural that Jesus should frame His allegory in language that had been used to describe the people of God under the old dispensation," explains R. V. G. Tasker, (*Tyndale Bible Commentary on John,* p. 173).

See the picture. Jesus is the true vine—the real one, not merely a type or symbol. God is the vine-dresser—the one who cares for the vineyard. We are the branches —our growth comes only through Jesus.

Christians have a close family relationship. It's not like the magician who was asked by a spectator, "Who taught you the trick of sawing a woman in half?"

"Oh, I've known how to do that since I was a child," he replied.

"Really!" the observer exclaimed. "Are you one of a large family?"

The magician replied with a smile, "I have several half-sisters."

There is a far closer relationship among God's people. All have the same Father. Without Him, we can do nothing (John 15:5). Separated from Him we are hopeless.

Paul described the condition like this: "Remember that you were at that time separate from Christ, excluded from the commonwealth of Israel, and strangers to the covenants of promise, having no hope and without God in the world" (Ephesians 2:12 NAS).

God made salvation possible through the atoning death of Jesus. Man must choose to accept and obey God's provision if he is to be a part of the vine. Peter explained it like this on Pentecost: "Repent, and be baptized every one of you in the name of Jesus Christ for the forgiveness of your sins; and you shall receive the gift of the Holy Spirit. . . . Save yourselves from this crooked generation" (Acts 2:38, 40 RSV).

## Characteristics

Jesus says that we must be fruitful. "Every branch in Me that does not bear fruit, He takes away; and every branch that bears fruit, He prunes it, that it may bear more fruit" (John 15:2 NAS). A plant should produce its own kind. If you plant a tomato seed, you expect to find on the branch a tomato, not an orange. God expects us to grow and be fruitful.

These fruits of the Spirit are the Christlike qualities which must be in our lives. Paul lists them as "love, joy, peace, patience, kindness, goodness, faithfulness, gentleness, self control" (Galatians 5:22, 23 NAS).

Once when Florence Nightingale was caring for a dying soldier, he looked at her gratefully and said, "You're Jesus Christ to me." This should be said to every Christian. "So then, you will know them by their fruits" (Matthew 7:20 NAS).

Paul told the Romans, "You have died to the law through the body of Christ, so that you may belong to another, to him who has been raised from the dead in order that we may bear fruit for God" (Romans 7:4 RSV). He explained that he wanted to preach in Rome, to help win souls, and build up saints—and he calls this process "reaping the harvest" (Romans 1:13).

Your life should show these fruits—the good motives, desires, attitudes, words, acts and dispositions. Does it? Höw is your life? What fruit are you bearing? How are you like your Father?

One teen-ager was discussing her report card with a friend. "No wonder Jean always gets an A in French," she grumbled. "Her father and mother speak French around the house."

Her boyfriend tried to console her. "Well, if that's so, I ought to get an A in geometry. My parents talk in circles."

That follows, doesn't it? We ought to be like our parents. Christians need to be like their Father also. Besides being fruitful, they must be faultless.

## Cleansing

The believer is cleansed. Jesus says, "You are already clean because of the word which I have spoken to you" (John 15:3 NAS). Cleansing comes by the Word. Not everyone who comes to church is a Christian. Not everyone who joins some religious group has truly committed his life to Jesus. "Everybody talkin' 'bout heaven ain't going there," as the old spiritual says.

Jesus explained this more fully as He alluded to Judas: "Not all of you are clean" (John 13:10, 11). One may have a close connection to Jesus and not be cleansed. One may outwardly appear to be one of His and not be. Judas did. But God doesn't look on the outward appearance.

Inner cleansing is what counts. This is the significance of Christian baptism. One may be immersed in water and it will do him no good unless he truly is a repentant believer. (See Mark 16:16, Acts 2:38.) But when he sincerely obeys Christ, Peter explains that "baptism now saves you—not the removal of dirt from the flesh, but an appeal to God for a good conscience—through the resurrection of Jesus Christ" (1 Peter 3:21 NAS).

During the furor of the Watergate scandal in 1973, Senator Barry Goldwater was asked, "What can be done to prevent another Watergate?" His incisive reply was, "Stop printing dollar bills. In other words, nothing —unless people suddenly become highly moral, honest, and ethical" (*Time,* May 28, 1973, p. 19).

This is it exactly. "For as he thinketh in his heart, so is he" (Proverbs 23:7 KJV). Freud said, "Thought is action in rehearsal." Faultless thinking is essential for faultless living. We cannot, of course, become faultless by ourselves. Jesus is the one who cleanses us and helps us toward perfection.

He requires that we be faithful also in our efforts. "Abide in Me, and I in you," Jesus commanded. He added, "Just as the Father has loved Me, I have also loved you; abide in my love" (John 15:4, 9 NAS). It's true that we are saved by God's grace. It's true that we cannot save ourselves. But our Lord has seen fit to place squarely upon our shoulders the responsibility of abiding in Christ. We must do this much. "Be faithful unto death, and I will give you the crown of life," reads Christ's promise (Revelation 2:10 NAS).

We must do our part. Are you doing yours? You need the honesty to see your responsibility in personal Christian growth and in fellowship with the local church.

It's easy to say, "If the preacher had more interesting sermons, I'd grow. If the Bible School teacher were better, I'd attend class. If I had more time, I'd read the Bible." But while we try to pass the buck, the finger of responsibility points back at us. Do you have the characteristics of a growing Christian?

## Conditions

In John 15:6-11, our Lord lays down the conditions of Christian growth. If we fail to abide in Him, five things will happen:

1. We will be thrown away.
2. We will wither.
3. We will be picked up.
4. We will be thrown into the fire.
5. We will be burned.

One may linger among the true believers for awhile, like Judas, but he finds no peace without the life Jesus gives. His punishment is not annihilation, but unending torment (Matthew 25:46). If you fail to accept Jesus, or if you accept Him and later renounce Him, or if you do not abide in Him, this is the fate that awaits.

But on the other hand, glorious results are yours if you do meet God's conditions. Jesus promises that your prayers will be effective (15:7), you will bear much fruit (15:8), and you will have fullness of joy (15:10).

Ask yourself if you can say with Paul, "I have been crucified with Christ: and I myself no longer live, but Christ lives in me. And the real life I now have within this body is a result of my trusting in the Son of God, who loved me and gave himself for me" (Galatians 2:20 LB).

## Grounded Faith for Growing Christians

Now that you've read this chapter, try these Scripture passages: John 15; Galatians 2.

# 6

# HOW TO
# GET
# TO HEAVEN

Dr. Will Herberg, a noted philosopher and social historian, was interviewed recently by *U.S. News and World Report* (June 4, 1973, beginning on p. 54). The Drew University professor assessed religion in the United States. He declared, "In numbers, the mass of American people are immersed in religiousness."

"Ninety-five per cent identify themselves as being Protestant, Catholic or Jew. About 70 per cent say they're members of churches. In 1972, the Gallup Poll reported, 40 per cent of American adults said they attended church or synagogue in a typical week."

But then Dr. Herberg made a pointed observation. "In content, however, this religiousness is becoming more and more vacuous, because religion has come to serve a new role in this country—a non-religious role, essentially. I mean religious 'belonging' has now become a primary form of self-identification and social location, the way of being an American."

It is just this "non-religious" type of religion that concerns the true Christian. All too much of that existed in

Jesus' day! He pointed it out. He told off the people who practiced it. He called them hypocrites, "play actors."

Throughout church history there have been the hangers-on—those who wanted to be called Christian without truly belonging to Christ. It just never has been possible.

Today we tend to equate being an American with being a Christian. Some people feel they're sure to go to Heaven because they attend church occasionally.

Others feel God will save them eecause they've been born in a Christian home. That is obviously false. Being born in a Christian home doesn't make you a Christian any more than being born in a garage makes you an automobile!

If we want to go to Heaven, the Bible tells us what to do.

## God's Grant

God has given us what we need. He has provided what we can't get for ourselves or by ourselves. Peter said, "His divine power has granted to us everything pertaining to life and godliness, through the knowledge of Him who called us by His own glory and excellence" (2 Peter 1:3 NAS).

If God has granted us all things that pertain to life and godliness, that doesn't leave much else! No one can say, "I'm going to Heaven because of all the good I've done." It doesn't work that way. First God must reveal himself and provide a way for you to learn of Him and follow Him.

The good news is that He has! It comes "through the knowledge of Him who called us." As you come to know Jesus through His Word, God is providing everything you need. This harmonizes with Paul's assurance that Scripture provides everything necessary "that the man of God may be adequate, equipped for every good work" (2 Timothy 3:17 RSV).

God's Son and God's Word offer total provision for us

to stand complete before God. "And this is eternal life, that they may know Thee, the only true God, and Jesus Christ whom Thou has sent" (John 17:3 NAS). Jesus said, "I came that they might have life, and might have it abundantly" (John 10:10).

Through this revelation, Peter adds that God has also granted us "His precious and magnificent promises" (2 Peter 1:4). These provide the way of escape from a worldly society and make us partakers of a heavenly nature.

## Man's Growth

The way to Heaven has two sides. God must do His part (and He has), but man must also do his. God first had to grant salvation—to make it possible. But He then required that man exert himself in full obedience to the heavenly offer.

Bengel compares 2 Peter 1:3-11 to the parable of the ten virgins. Five were wise; five were foolish. He noted that the flame represents what God imparts without our labor. "But the oil," he added, "is that which a man must pour into life by his own study and his own faithful effort, so that the flame may be fed and increased."

*You* have to do something. You must make an effort. Lincoln used to tell about the poor lady who always complained about her worthless husband. He would beat her; he would scold the children; he wouldn't work.

"Ah, be patient, sister," her minister instructed. "Set a good example and heap coals of fire on his head."

"Coals of fire wouldn't help," she responded. "I've already poured boilin' water on him and it didn't even take the dander out of his hair!"

Well, she tried to do something. Perhaps she was wrong, but at least she tried. So must we. For we don't grow into the kind of Christians we ought to be overnight. We need to think of that the next time we're tempted to "pour some boilin' water" on a Christian sister or brother who stumbles. Peter adds that we must apply diligence (2 Peter 1:5) in seeking Heaven.

Like an army advancing toward its objective, so the Christian must march steadily forward. Someone has said, "The Christian life must not be an initial spasm followed by chronic inertia." Instead it is a life of growth.

The apostle next lists the particular qualities we need:

For then you must learn to know God better and discover what he wants you to do. Next, learn to put aside your own desires so that you will become patient and godly, gladly letting God have his way with you. This will make possible the next step, which is for you to enjoy other people and to like them, and finally you will grow to love them deeply (2 Peter 1:5-7 LB).

F. R. Havergal has said, "Full consecration may in one sense be the act of a moment and in another the work of a lifetime. It must be complete to be real, and yet, if real it is always incomplete; a point of rest and yet a perpetual progression."

In one of the church papers that comes to my desk, I once noted an interesting article by the minister. It was titled: "Size Isn't Everything." Now that wasn't too strange. Many ministers who serve churches that aren't growing are quick to make that observation! Bragging about quality instead of quantity is far from Scriptural. We can have both in the church—as the book of Acts demonstrates!

Nevertheless the man who wrote the article isn't from a small, dormant church. In fact the congregation is one of the largest Christian churches in the country. The Los Gatos, California, church had 1558 present on the previous Sunday according to the newsletter. Here is what minister Marvin Rickard wrote:

Too many churches measure success in terms of 'beating last year's attendances' and 'meeting the budget.' If they do both things, all is well, the preacher gets calls to hold meetings, the church is looked up to by smaller churches, and the board is satisfied.

"Once I bit into a very large apple. It was as giant and red as could be. But inside it was pithy and dry. What a disappointment! It was bigger than most others, bigger than last year's crop and really an eye-pleaser.

"Being larger can be a handicap instead of an asset, you see. A church can add size without adding flavor. It can have every appearance of being nearly perfect but when you get beneath the surface, it's not all that good.

"People can get 'lost' in the crowd when membership is bigger. I am afraid that we have had quite a few 'joiners' here. Some folks think it is good to be a 'member' somewhere, and we're close! Some people like to have their children in Sunday school while the folks 'attend church' and our schedule allows this possibility. You can do it all in about an hour. 'Joiners' aren't interested in getting into a Sunday-school class on an adult level or attending on Sunday nights at all.

"A larger church can carry the financial burden of 'spiritual free-loaders.' These require seating, floor space, papers, heat, lights, parking, nurseries and all the rest, but they never put anything in the offering. Or if they do, it's parking meter change.

"Also in a larger 'apple' it's easier for a worm to hide. We may even have an uncoverted member or two ourselves, try as we might to hold the lines. They spoil the flavor because spiritual things are distasteful to them. They bring lower standards and cancel out real life.

"It doesn't have to be that way at all. It ought to be possible to be large and have solid flavor all the way through. This is our aim, not size. We long to see every believer growing in faith, service, and love for Christ. Loyalty ought to be, not to an organization, not to a group of friends, but to Christ. Our response ought to be out of love not duty. Let's do all we can to make sure that our size is an asset for the Lord."

God wants us to grow. Man must grow if he is to go to Heaven. The church must grow if she is to obey the Lord's commission. When men receive God's grant of salvation and seek to grow in Him, they enjoy a wonderful assurance.

## Your Gain

Peter outlined the benefits awaiting the faithful disciple:

> They render you neither useless nor unfruitful in the true knowledge of our Lord, . . . as long as you practice these things, you will never stumble; for in this way the entrance into the eternal kingdom of our Lord and Savior Jesus Christ will be abundantly supplied to you (2 Peter 1:8, 10, 11 NAS).

If we grow in Jesus, we'll bear the fruits of the Spirit in our lives. Progress is the way to more progress. If you want to be a better Christian, begin making those changes that you know should be made in your life. The poet sang:

> May every heart confess Thy name,
> And ever Thee adore,
> And, seeking Thee, itself inflame
> To seek Thee more and more.

"We would see Jesus," cried the Greeks. "He is the one we want." Peter says, "You will see Him, if you are zealous to make your calling and election sure."

Those who hold that there is nothing man can do for his salvation are forced to try to by-pass this text. Calvin said of it, "When the apostle requires these things, he by no means asserts they are in our power; but only shows what we ought to have and what ought to be done."

But is that the case? Look again at 2 Peter 1:5.

"Applying all diligence, in your faith supply. . ." Look at verse 10. "As long as you practice these things. . ." God isn't going to do this for us. He will help us, but we must do it. He will enable us, but we must grow.

As Wuest put it, "The divine nature is not an automatic self-propelling machine that will turn out a Christian life for the believer regardless of what that believer does or the attitude he takes toward the salvation God has provided." Indeed not. This is why Peter warns that if we are disobedient, we'll lose, not gain (verse 9).

Let us sing with Charles Wesley:
Soldiers of Christ, arise,
And put your armor on,
Strong in the strength which God supplies
Through his eternal Son.
Strong in the Lord of Hosts,
And in His mighty power,
Who in the strength of Jesus trusts
Is more than conqueror.

Stand, then, in His great might,
With all His strength endued;
And take, to arm you for the fight,
The panoply of God;
That, having all things done,
And all your conflicts past,
Ye may o'ercome thro' Christ alone,
And stand entire at last.

Leave no unguarded place,
No weakness of the soul,
Take every virtue, every grace,
And fortify the whole.
From strength to strength go on;
Wrestle, and fight, and pray;
Tread all the powers of darkness down,
And win the well fought day.

## Grounded Faith for Growing Christians

Now that you've read this chapter, try these Scripture passages: 1 Corinthians 3:1-9; 2 Peter 1:3-11.

# 7

# HELP SOMEONE GROW!

Calling all detective fans!

Consider today "the case of the disappearing convert." He is a typical new member of the church. He may have come through primary obedience to Christ, or he may have transferred membership.

First, here is his background. He visited the church a few times. He was contacted by the minister and some interested members. He was taught, his questions were answered. He kept coming—only to the morning service, however. Then he decided to be a part of the church.

Now what happens to this new convert?

Hopefully he will feel welcomed by the church. The minister will deliver his membership packet; an elder or deacon will stop to get acquainted with him. He will return his talent survey sheet. Soon he becomes active in the Bible-school class.

When a new members' class is offered, he attends each session. He offers to help when workers are needed. He begins attending on Sunday nights and Wednesday nights. He seeks to get to know others in the church. At fellowship dinners or picnics, he is present. He accepts a job in the church. Soon he feels a vital part of the growing church.

That's the way it should be.

But it doesn't always work out that well.

In the case of the disappearing convert, it is different. He became a Christian—or transferred membership—in much the same way as the man just described. But there things changed.

He never did get his talent sheet turned back in. The elder or deacon who was to visit and welcome him never made it by. The convert didn't feel he had time to stay for Bible school—and when he did stay, no one in the class spoke to him. They just sat and talked with their old cronies, and he sat alone feeling a little odd.

After a few weeks he mentioned how hard it was to get acquainted. He didn't speak to the people sitting by him in church—and they usually didn't greet him. Then the minister offended him by something he said.

The new members' class came at a time when he wanted to do something else, and so he only attended the first session. Someone from the church asked him to help usher, but he refused. He began finding it easier to miss a Sunday with no twinge of conscience. Finally, three months after he had became a part of the church, one of the members asked the preacher, "Whatever happened to so-and-so?"

And there you have him—the disappearing convert.

Whose fault is it when a new convert disappears?

His own?

Partly.

The church's?

I think we must say yes. It's true that each of us must give an account of himself before God. And it's true that the disappearing convert needed more personal commitment to Jesus; he needed more effort. But he also needed something else.

He needed other people. People who care. You need them too. And so do I. "No man is an island." We need others to help us. The church must meet men's needs.

Whose fault is it when a convert disappears?

We might as well ask, "Who is to blame when a baby dies of malnutrition or exposure?" Babes in Christ need tender, loving care, too. They need the milk of the Word, the warmth of Christian fellowship, and the security of the church's closeness. God has made them this way. Each Christian has a responsibility to help every other Christian. And that is your challenge: Help someone grow! Paul tells us what is involved in Ephesians 4.

## Various Roles (verse 11)

God has made us all different. While Christians have the great heritage of the faith in common, they are still individuals. Francis Foulkes reminds us that believers "may not expect their personalities, their gifts and their tasks to be all alike. In His wisdom, and to make each dependent on others, God has ordained not uniformity, but an endless variety of gifts for the members of the body."

Paul outlines here those present in the New Testament church. "And his gifts were that some should be apostles, some prophets, some evangelists, some pastors and teachers" (Ephesians 4:11 RSV).

No one dare look down on another who has a different gift or ability from his own. He is no better than any other. Neither is he any *less* important than any other. An elder in a church where I once preached would often pray, "And God, help us to remember that it takes every one of us—from the greatest to the least—to make this church go forward." He was right. To the Romans, the apostle explained it like this:

"For by the grace given to me I bid every one among you to think with sober judgment, each according to the measure of faith which God has assigned him. For as in one body we have many members, and all the members do not have the same function, so we, though many, are one body in Christ, and individually members one of another. Having gifts that differ according to the grace given to us, let us use them: if prophecy, in proportion to our faith; if service, in our serving; he who teaches, in his teaching; he who exhorts, in his exhortation; he who contributes, in liberality; he who gives aid, with zeal; he who does acts of mercy, with cheerfulness" (Romans 12:3-8 RSV).

There are various roles. Wherever you are, whatever ability you have, whatever the circumstances, there is something you can do for God. Several years ago I baptized a little grandmother—a lady in her eighties. She was as faithful as could be. She's worked with a ladies service group making clothing for the needy; she would share her social security check with the Lord; she would seldom miss a service.

Then her health began to fail. She was admitted to a nursing home. And when I would visit her there, she told me how she passed her copies of the *Lookout* and other Christian literature around to the other residents and the nurses.

Her eyes never lost their twinkle. She smiled at me one day and said, "Perhaps there is my place of service." And it was. She lived there until her death. And she made it a place of *service.* You can do that too.

## Singular Goal (verse 12)

Despite all of these varied offices in the church—they have but one purpose. "To equip the saints for the work of ministry, for building up the body of Christ" (Ephesians 4:12 RSV). Note that there should be no comma after the word "saints." It is to equip all of the saints for their work of ministry. You are a minister if you are a Christian. At the assembly on the Lord's day, you can be equipped for your work of ministry in the week ahead.

As Numbers 11:29 says, "Would that all the Lord's

people were prophets!'' Attendance at church should be not only a means of adoration of God, but also a time of participation with others, and preparation for service. We cannot hire trained professionals to do our Christian work for us. They can help equip us—but we all have a ministry. Our work must be designed to help others grow.

There are so many things you can do. You can teach. You can sing. You can call. You can be an usher, a greeter, a typist, an artist, a photographer, a janitor—or even work in the nursery! You are needed in the church. More important, you need to be doing something for God. You are needed. We all need each other.

A preacher told of seeing a paralyzed woman and a blind man who illustrated the lesson of mutual help. The crippled lady supplied eyes for the blind man, and the blind man used his feet to aid the lame. Imagine seeing them leave the church and cross the street in traffic. In her wheelchair, she used her eyes to look for the green light. He in turn used his legs to push her across the street.

Paul put it like this: ''And the eye cannot say unto the hand, I have no need of thee; nor again the head to the feet, I have no need of you'' (1 Corinthians 12:21).

We need each other. We need to help each other grow. A missionary described an unforgettable scene. He says, ''I once came upon two lepers who were planting seeds in a field. One leper had no fingers, and his hands were almost entirely wasted away. The other leper, who had no feet, but a good pair of hands, was being carried on the back of the first one. As they moved along, the man being carried was dropping seeds one by one into depressions made by the feet of his partner. By themselves each would have been helpless; but they were workers to- gether.'' So are we.

Have you been helping someone grow? That's our goal as Christians. You'll never know how much that brief visit to one in the hospital will mean. You may never know the worth of that dish of food taken to one who is sick; that card sent to one who has lost a loved one; that letter mailed to a lonely soldier or student. Even just a kindly word may help.

This is our goal—the building up of the body of Christ—helping someone grow. Paul shows us finally that in addition to various roles with a singular goal, we are to become mature souls.

## Mature Souls (verses 13-16)

Paul lists two basic goals in our quest for Christian maturity. They are:

1. To attain the unity of the faith.

This oneness of believers is a special concern of those of us in the Christian church.

2. To attain the knowledge of the Son of God; the measure of the stature of the fullness of Christ. "Be like Jesus, this my song," said the poet. "O to be like Thee, blessed Redeemer." The goal of our lives must be the example of Jesus. This, too, assures that we help someone grow. For that's what He did.

Mature Christians are not led astray by every radio preacher; by every front-door religious salesman; by every television mystic.

So that we may no longer be children, tossed to and fro and carried about with every wind of doctrine, by the cunning of men, by their craftiness in deceitful wiles. Rather, speaking the truth in love, we are to grow up in every way into him who is the head, into Christ (Ephesians 4:14, 15 RSV). We need to grow in our knowledge of the Word.

Our personal, spiritual growth comes from the help other Christians give as well as our own effort. "From whom the whole body, joined and knit together by every joint with which it is supplied, when each part is working properly, makes bodily growth and upbuilds itself in love" (Ephesians 4:16 RSV).

Charles L. Allen put his finger on the problem of our society a few years ago. He declared that Madison Avenue has been saying, "If you want to be happy, if you want an abundant life, the way to accomplish it is to get the right kind of automobile, television set, washing machine, electric refrigerator. If you get enough of these mechanical things, life to you will be a happy experience."

"And," he charged, "America has been sold on that idea; we've swapped God for gadgets." But eventually, he went on, "something will happen that you're not prepared for.

"You can't meet a crisis with a Cadillac; you can't mend a broken heart with a washing machine; you can't lift the burden of a conscience with a vacuum cleaner. Something happens and we don't have anything inside to face it with, and that's where we develop a lot of these neuroses, tensions, problems, and hurts."

He is right, of course. People are more important than machines. People are more important even than church-related institutions and programs. To God, people are everything. He sent Jesus to save people. He loves people. And he calls on us to love them too.

## Grounded Faith for Growing Christians

Now that you've read this chapter, try these Scripture passages: Ephesians 4, Philippians 3:12-16; 1 John 3:1-3.

# 8

# WHEN THE GROWING GETS ROUGH

It's easy enough to be pleasant,
When life flows by like a song;
But the man worthwhile
Is the man who can smile
When everything goes dead wrong.

I'd have to agree with the poet. Until you've had some problems or difficulties in your life, it's going to be hard for you to have proper perspective. After you go through hours of trial, things look different. "Some of the sharpest pictures are developed in the darkest rooms."

Maybe you feel in a place like that now. It could be due to sickness, the death of one you love, family difficulties, trouble at work. Whatever it is, you feel deep within that the going is pretty rough. Consider what Paul said about this experience.

In writing the Corinthians, he makes high claims about the Christian ministry. Then he anticipates an objection the readers may raise. Someone may assert that the humiliation and suffering Paul has endured refute the idea that he can be God's ambassador. He answers, as McGarvey explains, that "God put the treasure in an earthen vessel in order that the survival of the perishing vessel when subjected to all manner of (difficulty) might prove the value, in the sight of God, of the treasure within it."

You and I are simply earthen vessels. Not beautiful, ornate golden containers; we're just clay pots. But in God's sight, there's something special about man. He has a soul. He lives eternally. He has a personal responsibility before his Maker. Because of this, the changing conditions of life can be seen in true perspective.

## Difficult Reactions (2 Corinthians 4:8, 9)

They tell of a newly-rich woman who wanted to impress her friends at a dinner party. All was prepared for a swanky evening. There was only one problem—her new false teeth. The upper plate kept slipping down. So she told her new butler about the problem. "Tompkins, if this plate begins to slip while I'm talking, I may not realize it. So if you should see that happen, just come over and say to me, 'Mr. Jones is at the door.'" As the evening progressed, her fears were realized.

Tompkins dutifully came up and said, "Mr. Jones is at the door." But she was going on so, bragging to her friends, that she didn't pay attention.

A few minutes later she realized that the butler had been trying to get her attention. "Did you say something, Tompkins?" she asked.

"Yes, madam. I said that Mr. Jones was at the door —but he's in the noodle soup now."

That's when the going gets rough!

But these little problems that upset us are nothing compared to what happened to Paul.

They tried to kill him in Damascus and again in Jerusalem. They drove him out of Antioch. They attempted to stone him in Iconium. They did stone him and left him for dead in Lystra. At Philippi they beat him and put him in the stocks. He was frequently the victim of plots and mob violence. (He summed up some of his problems in 2 Corinthians 11:23-27.)

What about you? Are you in the midst of difficult reactions? When the growing gets rough, what do you do? How can you make it through? Some turn to liquor; some have nowhere to turn and decide to end it all. But the Christian *has* a place to go. "Where could I go but to the Lord?" Paul shows us that, when there are difficult reactions, we have divine resources.

## Divine Resources (2 Corinthians 4:7, 10, 11)

Comedian Joey Adams asked Ethel Waters about the changes in her life. From the "stormy weather" of poverty, overweight, and weariness, she had changed to a gay, vibrant person. She explained, "God has so many goodies for everybody, and He puts them all in front of you. All you have to do is bend down and pick them up—and that's just what I did. You see, I've never been that far away from God that I can't reach Him when I need Him."

"What was the greatest single influence in your life?" he asked in the interview (*Family Weekly,* March 25, 1973, p. 4).

"There has been only one," she answered. "Prayer."

Divine resources!

"We are sore pressed at every point but not hemmed in. There are all kinds of pressure on us, but we are never in so tight a corner that there is no way out. It is the characteristic of the Christian life that there is always an element of spaciousness in it," explains William Barclay.

We must remember that the power is of God and not ourselves. The remarkable testimonies from P.O.W.'s released from Viet Nam point to the spiritual strength that sustained them in captivity. When the going gets rough, don't forget Jesus. He is always willing to help you.

The amazing thing is that through these difficult reactions, with the help of divine resources, we can endure. (Paul explains this in 2 Corinthians 12:7-10.)

God uses people to help people also. You are one of these divine resources. It may be that there is a brother or sister facing a real trial just now—and you can help. God will use your loving concern to strengthen that one.

The name Roy Regal may be remembered by older sports fans. In the 1929 Rose Bowl Game, he was the California player who got the ball, became confused, and ran the sixty-five yards in the wrong direction, losing the game for his team. Friends who heard him describe the incident say that he went all to pieces when he realized what he'd done.

He ran from the field to the dressing room in shame and humiliation. Between halves he was lying there so disgusted with himself that he fully planned to take his life after his teammates returned to the field. Then the coach called his name, "Roy."

"Yes, sir."

"Roy, when you go in this half, I want . . ."

"Me, sir? I can't."

The coach put his arm around Roy's shoulder. His teammates gathered round. "Roy, I know how you feel. But is game is only half over, you know."

Roy did play the second half—and next year was captain of the team. Now a schoolteacher in a western city, he stated, "It was that hand on my shoulder in the darkest moment of my life that saved my life. It gave me a faith in my fellow man that nothing will ever shake."

From difficult reactions, with divine resources, God provides daily renewal.

## Daily Renewal (2 Corinthians 4:16)

Isn't it strange how we grow from our hardships and problems if we accept them in the right way? An athlete forces himself to go through strenuous exercise, hard practice sessions, long hours of rigorous effort. Then he finds increased ability and gives an impressive performance when he is in the game.

Sometimes in the game of life, it gets hard for us. We feel like we're not getting the breaks; things go wrong; there are some "bad calls" by the officials; "the crowd" turns against us. What do you do then? Athletes have a saying, "When the going gets tough, the tough get going." The title of this chapter is an adptation of that: when the *growing* gets rough. We grow by tough experiences.

When you reach the point that your prayer life is hard to keep constant, when it's easier to stay home on Sunday than assemble for worship, when daily Bible reading seems like a chore—what do you do? When the growing gets tough, when you have difficult reactions, look to the divine resources. If you do, you'll find daily renewal.

After all, Jesus faced problems. He endured afflictions. In them and through them, you can feel Christ's presence with you. Jesus turns deadly afflictions into triumphant victory. The "fellowship of His sufferings" is the way Paul describes it.

Really what does it matter if we have a few hours, or days, or months, or even years of hardship here?

For this slight momentary affliction is preparing for us an eternal weight of glory beyond all comparison, because we look not to the things that are seen but to the things that are unseen; for the things that are seen are transient, but the things that are unseen are eternal (2 Corinthians 4:17, 18 RSV).

Consider the wealth of meaning behind Paul's use of this phrase "our light affliction" to describe all that he himself had gone through. Surely you haven't had things worse than Paul. Look what he endured. Look how he viewed it.

Sufferings that weaken the body may be the very ones that strengthen the soul.

A black student at Fisk University in Nashville was on

board a steamer that caught fire. He fastened life pre-servers on his wife and himself. In the panic, as people tried to save themselves, someone tore his wife's pre-server from her. She was helpless in the water.

She clung to her husband, her hands on his shoulders, trying to remain afloat. Soon her strength was exhausted. "I can't hold on any longer," she cried.

"Try a little bit more," he pleaded. Then he added, "Let's sing, 'Rock of Ages.' "

Immediately they began to sing faintly. Others in the water heard them. One by one the nearly exhausted swimmers would raise their heads above the waves and join in the prayer: "Rock of Ages, cleft for me, Let me hide myself in Thee."

Strength returned and sustained them until a lifeboat could rescue them.

God does not solve all our problems for us. He does not remove them. But, if we share them with Him, He gives us the strength to endure. When the growing gets rough, don't forget Jesus.

## Grounded Faith for Growing Christians

Now that you've read this chapter, try these Scripture passages: 1 Corinthians 2:1-5; 2 Corinthians 4:7-16.

# 9

# THE HOLY SPIRIT HELPS US GROW

Words mean different things to different people. Take the word "strike," for example. To a bowler, it's great news. To a batter in a baseball game, it isn't. It means one thing when you're lighting a match and another when you're picketing for the union.

Likewise the Holy Spirit means different things to different people. When people speak of the Spirit today, some refer only to charismatic activity. Others assert a leading they sense in the ecumenical movement. Still others mean simply a feeling or impulse they have. Far more accurate and decidedly more crucial is what the Bible tells us of God's Spirit.

Once again, it is good news in the gospel. Jesus introduces the Spirit as a friend, a comforter, an attorney, a companion, and a partner in all that is good. The Holy Spirit helps us grow to be like Jesus. He aids in several ways.

## Through God's Word (John 16:12-15)

A common mistake is to read these verses as if Jesus

said them to us today. When He declared, "He will guide you into all the truth, . . . He will disclose to you what is to come" (John 16:13 NAS), our Lord was speaking to the apostles. The truth into which they were miraculously guided is available to us in the Bible.

I find no Scripture which assures me that the Holy Spirit is going to lead me by some magical, mystical way into truth that is hidden from another believer.

Jesus promised that the Spirit would guide the apostles into all truth. The Spirit did just that. The writings of these inspired men were preserved from error. What they spoke and wrote we have available in God's Word. In this way, the Holy Spirit guides us today and helps us grow.

Whenever we are tempted to sidestep the occasional difficult passages of the Old Testament, we must recall that the Spirit was speaking there, too. He was preparing the world for Christ's coming (see 1 Peter 1:10, 11; 2 Peter 1:21).

During Christ's earthly ministry the Spirit demonstrated to all that this indeed was God's Son (Luke 3:22). Jesus was filled with the Spirit and aided by the Spirit in all His works.

When the Master came to His last night, He promised the disciples, "But the Helper, the Holy Spirit, whom the Father will send in My name, He will teach you all things, and bring to your remembrance all that I said to you" (John 14:26 NAS).

This verse explains why the writings of Peter, or John, or Paul, or any other inspired writer, are of equal authority with the words of Jesus himself. The Spirit spoke through them. Our basis of faith is a God-breathed book. The Spirit works through the Word, although not through the Word alone.

When you want to learn God's will and to have the Spirit exercise greater control over you, turn to the Word. This is the source of growth.

A woman with this problem wrote to Ann Landers:

I am all mixed up. I am in my very early 20's and engaged to marry a man I thought I knew well. Now I discover he has been lying about a few things. He said he was 27, has 2 children and was divorced two years ago. He is actually 36, has six children and is still married.

Need I tell you I was shocked? But I still love him and can't give him up.

I am trying to get my family to be forgiving Christians and accept this man, but they stubbornly refuse to discuss it. I have been going to church regularly and praying for divine guidance but so far I haven't received it. Help me, please.                                    —Love him

Dear Love: My answer is in your letter. It's the second sentence.

The reason you aren't getting any "divine guidance" is that you and the Lord are on different wave lengths. He's on the side of the wife and six kids.

Self-will and prejudice may blind us to the leading of the Lord. We must turn to His Work with an open mind and humble spirit if we are to experience the leading of His Spirit.

Maritime history tells how the brave, seafaring Norsemen sailed without aid of compass. They carried crates of ravens aboard each ship. When there was any doubt as to direction, they would release a raven. They watched it fly higher and higher. They would then follow, knowing it would go to the nearest land. When we are uncertain in life, we have but to follow the direction of the Spirit through the Word. He will always lead us to God.

## Through Our Inner Thoughts
## (Romans 8:26, 27)

The Spirit works inside each Christian. Jesus assured us that the Holy Spirit would convict men of sin (John 16:7-11). To "convict" means both to prove or find guilty and also to convince one of his own wrongdoing or error.

Perhaps His work in pointing out our faults to us is comparatively easy. We certainly can see the other fellow's faults quick enough! But there is a difference between finding someone guilty and making him feel personally responsible and repentant for his wrongdoing.

The Spirit works on our thoughts. When we read or hear God's Word, the Spirit will tell us what is wrong with our life. Then one of two things will happen. Either we'll quit reading the Bible and going to church—or else we can pray like the publican, "Lord, be merciful to me, a sinner," and then change our ways. In that way, we grow.

The Spirit also helps us in prayer. Paul said,

The Spirit also helps our weakness; for we do not know how to pray as we should, but the Spirit Himself intercedes for us with groanings too deep for words; and He who searches the hearts knows what the mind of the Spirit is, because He intercedes for saints according to the will of God (Romans 8:26, 27 NAS).

The Spirit helps us grow into mature Christians. The spiritual man is trusting Jesus to live the Christian life in him through the Holy Spirit. Christ in you *is* the hope of glory! The Spirit brings us into Christ (John 3:5; Acts 2:38). The Spirit lives in the believer's heart (Galatians 4:6). The same mighty power that brought Jesus from the tomb is available to the Christian (Romans 8:11). Working within, the Spirit helps you grow.

## Through Our Outer Acts
## (Galatians 5:16-25)

The Spirit manifests divine nature in us (2 Peter 1:3, 4). God's Spirit is in us—in control of, or in place of, our spirits. This is the ultimate goal. As Seth Wilson said, "This is the end for which miracles were wrought; it is the object for which miracles can never be an acceptable substitute."

God is more concerned about a Christlike quality produced by the Spirit in your life than with your "speaking in tongues" or any other alleged Spirit-produced phenomenon. (Read Galatians 5:16-25).

In addition, the Spirit helps us find victorious Christian living (Romans 8:13-17). If you are a child of God, you should bear a family resemblance. Can a person look at your life and tell you are a Christian? Do friends, family, and associates see something different with you? They will, if God's Spirit is in your heart.

An old song, "Doin' What Comes Naturally," describes the contrast. God's Spirit helps you do what doesn't come naturally—the hard, difficult choices that are evident in the life of a disciplined believer.

The Spirit helps you turn the other cheek; the Spirit helps you keep your mouth closed instead of snapping back; the Spirit helps you be honest when you see a chance to cheat. These are fruits of the Spirit. They are qualities of life which He produces.

Some children were asking their father about the Holy Spirit at family devotions one day. "How can we believe in Him when no one has seen Him?" they asked.

Their father found he couldn't explain it satisfactorily, so he arranged to take them on a tour of a local electric power plant.

As they stood there before the throbbing generators, he said, "Now, boys, I want this to help explain the Holy Spirit's power to you. From these generators we get the power to light our lights, heat our stove, operate the TV, and run our furnace. Now do you see electricity here?"

They quickly admitted that they did not.

"Then," said the father, "if you can't see it, it must not be here."

One boy got the idea quickly. "We can't see it, but we sure know what it does."

"That's the way it is with the Holy Spirit," their father concluded. "Although we have not seen Him, we know of His power because we can see what He does in the lives of men."

Moody described the burial of an aged saint—poor in this world's goods, but rich in heavenly treasure. The men from the funeral home served as pallbearers. They were hurrying a little as they went to the grave, wanting to get the service over with. The minister quietly told them, "Tread softly. You are carrying a temple of the Holy Spirit."

Whenever you see a Christian, there is a temple of God's Spirit. Paul explained,

Do you not know that your body is a temple of the Holy Spirit who is in you, whom you have from God, and that you are not your own? For you have been bought with a price: therefore glorify God in your body (1 Corinthians 6:19, 20 NAS).

Is this what your life shows to the world?

Not only does the Holy Spirit help us grow, but He guarantees our hope of heaven. "You were sealed in Him with the Holy Spirit of promise, who is given as a pledge of our inheritance" (Ephesians 1:13, 14 NAS).

## Grounded Faith for Growing Christians

Now that you've read this chapter, try these Scripture passages: John 16:12-15; Romans 8:26, 27; Galatians 5:16-25.

# 10

# HIGHER GROUND

Christians are like mountain climbers. They must always strive for higher ground. We can sing with Johnson Oatman:

I'm pressing on the upward way,
New heights I'm gaining ev'ry day;
Still praying as I onward bound,
'Lord, plant my feet on higher ground.'

In Colossians 3, the apostle outlines how Christians can grow.

## Put Your Mind on Things Above (v. 1-4)

The chapter's opening verses are more logically attached to the preceding section. They remind us not to be held by earthly rules and human limitations, but to be subject solely to Jesus Christ.

"If then you have been raised up with Christ, keep seeking the things above, where Christ is, seated at the right hand of God. Set your mind on the things above, not on the things that are on earth" (Colossians 3:1, 2 NAS).

Obviously filth and smut exist on every hand. One need not be a Puritan to be upset about present magazines, movies, and mores. How is the Christian to meet trash that too often fills the television screen and newsstand rack? Scripture tells us it must begin with our mind.

A. T. Robertson points out, "There are bad smells in every city, but only one with depraved nostrils seeks them out and revels in them like a sewer rat or hyena. Some modern artists and novelists call this realism, and thus justify the slime that they parade to the public. But most of all, they reveal their own depraved mind given over to uncleanness."

A teacher in our high school had a greater influence on me than she probably ever knew. I never had a class under her. I didn't know her well. I had always thought of her as a little eccentric—wrapped up in her Latin and history classes.

During my senior year, some of us put on an assembly that was just a lot of clowning around. I wrote one of the skits. I thought it was really funny. The kids ate it up.

But later word got to me that this teacher, Miss McGowan, had been a little upset about it. She had reportedly thought some of the lines were in poor taste.

I decided that I'd just go talk to her about it. I wasn't afraid of her! And, after all, what was so bad about the skit?

I'll never forget that afternoon I went to her room at the end of the school day. I waited until she finished talking with some of her students. Then I walked over to her desk.

"Miss McGowan," I began, "I heard you didn't like my skit in the assembly. I wanted to know what was wrong with it."

She was very calm. She *had* been bothered by it, she explained. But she didn't start bawling me out.

"But there wasn't anything really bad or wrong in it," I defended.

She stood quietly and said, "No, Sam, that may be true. But there is so much to see in life that's good. Why focus on anything but the good? There's a poem," she mused. "It goes: 'Two men stood behind prison bars—One saw mud, the other stars.' "

That was about all there was to our conversation. But I've never forgotten it. It made me see the crucial importance of one's outlook—or perhaps I should say his *uplook.*

When we concentrate on things above, we demonstrate a life hid with Christ in God. We anticipate also our reward in glory. This is the renewal of our mind (Romans 12:1).

My heart has no desire to stay
When doubts arise and fears dismay;
Tho' some may dwell where these abound,
My prayer, my aim is higher ground.

## Put Off Earthly Habits (v. 5-11)

"Therefore consider the members of your earthly body as dead to immorality, impurity, passion, evil desire, and greed, which amounts to idolatry" (Colossians 1:5 NAS).

Paul goes on to outline other old habits to be put aside: anger, wrath, malice, slander, abusive speech and lying (v. 8, 9).

Too often we don't realize the damaging effect of just one sin. We rationalize, "This is just once. It won't hurt. I can get by with it." Yet, as Spurgeon pointed out, "There was but one crack in the lantern, but the wind found it and blew out the candle. How great a mischief one unguarded point of character may cause for us. One leak sank the vessel and all on board drowned. One wound may kill the body and one destroy the soul."

You may have known Christians who were good, fine people for many years. Then came one incident. One night. It ruined their reputation, their influence, their life. Don't let that happen to you. Put off the habits of the past.

Jesus warned, "And if your right eye makes you stumble, tear it out, and throw it from you; for it is better for you that one of the parts of your body perish, than for your whole body to be thrown into hell" (Matthew 5:29 NAS).

The sins listed by Paul in Colossians 3 may be classified as three types:

1. Sensualism
2. Pride
3. Unbrotherly division.

We must shed these habits like an old tattered garment "For it is on account of these things that the wrath of God will come," Paul warns (3:6). God will not tolerate sin. You may fool others, but you don't fool God. Instead the Christian is to live a renewed life (verse 10). It calls for courage to stand for righteousness and truth in an ungodly world.

General Grant and his staff were gathered in a farmhouse in Virginia, back in the Civil War days. Several officers were standing by the fireplace. He was alone in the corner, apparently in deep thought.

One officer said, "I've got a story for you men." To indicate what was coming, he added, "I believe I can tell it since there are no ladies present."

An expectant ripple of laughter went through the room. General Grant stood and remarked quietly, "No, but there are gentlemen here." The story was never told.

Some who would not tell an impure story think nothing of listening to one. When temptation comes, followers of Jesus must put off earthly habits.

I want to live above the world,
Tho' Satan's darts at me are hurled;
For faith has caught the joyful sound,
The song of saints on higher ground.

## Put On Christlike Character (v. 12-17)

It's not enough to quit doing wrong. The Christian must start doing right. In one of his frequent listings of

Christian graces, Paul points out how we should live:

Put on a heart of compassion, kindness, humility, gentleness and patience, bearing with one another, and forgiving each other, whoever has a complaint against any one; just as the Lord forgave you, so also should you. And beyond all these things put on love, which is the perfect bond of unity (Colossians 3:12-14 NAS).

How do we become like this? By letting Christ rule in our hearts (verse 15), by having His Word within (verse 16), and by testing all behavior to make it pleasing to Him (verse 17).

"Whatever you do in word or deed, do all in the name of the Lord Jesus" (verse 17). What a motto! It is reminiscent of Charles Sheldon's famous novel, *In His Steps.* What powerful changes come when men resolve to ask, "What would Jesus do?"

How can you "put on a Christlike character"? Here are some practical suggestions:

1. Have Christian pictures, posters, plaques, mottos, Bible verses, etc. on the walls of your room and home.

2. Play Christian music on your record or tape player. Listen to cassettes of Bible studies, sermons, music, etc. If you're in your car a lot, this is a great chance. Some have purchased the New Testament on tape and regularly hear it while driving.

3. Choose Christian radio and television programs when possible. Be selective about other viewing.

4. Read good literature. Christian paperbacks make first-class reading available. The entire series of New Life Books offers you a chance to consider vital Bible themes in a popular, readable form. Subscribe to Christian periodicals, too.

5. God's Word itself is the final source of help both for educating and motivating. Daily Bible reading can make you a growing Christian. A free calendar to help you do this may be obtained by writing: Bible Memory Association, Box 12000, St. Louis, Mo. 63112. Seek to memorize Scripture. Be able to say with the psalmist, "Thy word

have I hid in mine heart'' (Psalm 119:11).

"Finally, brethren, whatever is true, whatever is honorable, whatever is right, whatever is pure, whatever is lovely, whatever is of good repute, if there is any excellence and if anything worthy of praise, let your mind dwell on these things" (Philippians 4:8, NAS).

A young man was away at college and his mother came for an unexpected visit. She was disappointed to see several centerfold pictures from *Playboy* on the walls of his room. She didn't say anything though. While in town she purchased a copy of the famous Sallman's head of Christ painting. She asked if she might put it up in his room and, with his permission, did.

On her next visit, that picture was still there in a prominent place, but the others were gone. Her son looked at her and explained, "When He went up, the others had to come down."

This is what it means to put on Christlike character. By following God's plan, we can reach higher ground!

I want to scale the utmost height,
And catch a gleam of glory bright;
But still I'll pray till heav'n I've found,
'Lord, lead me on to higher ground.'

Lord, lift me up and let me stand,
By faith, on heaven's tableland,
A higher plane than I have found;
Lord, plant my feet on higher ground.

## Grounded Faith for Growing Christians

Now that you've read this chapter, try these Scripture passages: Philippians 4:4-9; Colossians 3.

# 11

# TESTED FAITH

An avid sportsman bought a new retriever and took him out duck hunting. From his blind, the man shot a duck. The bird fell. The dog skipped right out on the water, tiptoed over, picked up the duck, and brought it back. He looked at the dog. *I couldn't have seen that right,* he thought.

So he fired again. Another duck fell. Again the dog skimmed out over the water, tiptoed, and came back with the duck. "Boy! That's something!" he exclaimed.

He called to a friend in a nearby blind. "Hey, Jim, did you see that?'

"Yep," acknowledge the other hunter.

"Well what about that? Don't you see something remarkable about my dog?"

"Sure do," replied his friend. "Your dog can't swim."

That's the way it is. It all depends on how you look at it. Life is like that—expecially in some of the serious moments we all face.

From the letter of James, let me direct your attention to some guidelines for growing in times of difficulty:

> Count it all joy, my brethren, when you meet various trials, for you know that the testing of your faith produces steadfastness. And let steadfastness have its full effect, that you may be perfect and complete, lacking in nothing (James 1:2-4 RSV).

James is known as the "practical epistle." While all New Testament books are helpful for everyday life, none is more relevant than James when we come to grips with honest problems and desperate needs.

Three things are taught here about tested faith:

## Requires Trials

What the King James Version renders "temptations" in verse 2 is better translated "trials." It speaks of the misfortunes that visit every home. It describes times of testing. It is "temptation," in a sense, but temptation directed to the end that the one tested grow stronger and purer through it.

The same word is used of a bird who "tests" his wings. The Queen of Sheba came to "test" the wisdom of Solomon. God was said to "test" Abraham when He appeared to be demanding Isaac's life. In this sense, we all are tested.

Such trials put your religion to the test. They ask, "Is it genuine? Are you *certain* of the faith that you talk about?"

C. S. Lewis noted that such times check the validity of our pious-sounding words. Speaking after the death of his wife, he declared:

> "You never know how much you really believe anything until its truth or falsehood becomes a matter of life and death to you. It is easy to say you believe a rope to be strong and sound as long as you are merely using it to cord a box. But suppose you had to hang by that rope over a precipice. Wouldn't you then first discover how much you really trusted it?"

Then he referred directly to his wife's death: "If my house had collapsed at one blow, that is because it was a house of cards" *(A Grief Observed,* Seabury Press, pp. 21, 31.)

When you meet trials, your faith is tested. Griefs, heart-aches, unpleasant moments, hours of hardship—all can serve to strengthen faith. Peter described the process like this:

> In this you greatly rejoice, even though now for a little while, if necessary, you have been distressed by various trials, that the proof of your faith, being more precious than gold which is perishable, even though tested by fire, may be found to result in praise and glory and honor at the revelation of Jesus Christ (1 Peter 1:6, 7 NAS).

So when trials come, don't gripe about them. Instead, rejoice! How much James sounds like Jesus! Constantly correcting our false sense of values, he shows us truth and reality. Jesus began His Sermon on the Mount by emphasizing the same type of unexpected evaluations:

> Blessed are those who are persecuted for righteousness' sake, for theirs is the kingdom of heaven. Blessed are you when men revile you and persecute you and utter all kinds of evil against you falsely on my account. Rejoice and be glad, for your reward is great in heaven, for so men persecuted the prophets who were before you (Matthew 5:10-12 RSV).

This is no whistling in the dark. Jesus met trial and temptation (see Matthew 4). So will we. Although we do not seek trouble, we find that it arrives anyway! The Christian need not fear. He accepts it with joy, faith, and increased dependence upon God. We can fight tempta-tion, and we can win. Jesus did. He assures us a way of escape (1 Corinthians 10:13).

As you sail along the Hudson River, you reach a place where you seem to be entirely hemmed in by hills. Ahead it looks as if the boat will crash into a rocky wall. Just as you come within the shadow of the mountain, an opening suddenly comes into view. The boat passes into one of the grandest bays of the river.

So it is with trials. When we meet them, we must go straight ahead, though we see no way out. Spiros

Zodhiates explains, "The way will reveal itself in due time if we keep on in the way of the Lord. And, as in the river the beautiful bay lies just around the frowning rock, so often the sweetest and best experience in life lies just beyond the most threatening temptation."

## Reaches Maturity

Only tested faith can reach maturity. James explains. "The testing of your faith produces endurance" (1:3). It leads to steadfastness; it breeds fortitude. Trials can develop unswerving constancy in faith despite adversity.

What happens to you under pressure? Do you get hot under the collar—and then explode? Do you run away and try to escape? Do you turn to liquor—or drugs—or sex—or travel—or any of a thousand other things—and try to forget? James says that tested faith develops staying power. It stands fast. It grows up.

Watch the welder as he works with a piece of iron. He holds it in the fire to soften it and make it pliable. This is why God permits our faith to be tested. Through these experiences, God can reshape us according to His image. Phillips translates Romans 12:2 like this: "Don't let the world around you squeeze you into its own mold, but let God remold your minds from within, so that you may prove in practice that the plan of God for you is good, meets all his demands and moves toward the goal of true maturity."

It was the Christians' endurance that amazed the heathen in the centuries of persecution. Those early martyrs did not die grimly. They died singing. One smiled in the flame. An incredulous guard demanded, "What do you find to smile at here?"

The Christian replied, "I saw the glory of God and was glad."

Patience helps us reach maturity. James adds, "And let endurance have its perfect result, that you may be perfect and complete, lacking in nothing" (1:4 NAS). Perfection is our goal. This doesn't mean we'll achieve it.

But endurance through testing lets patience have her "perfect work." She can do a thorough job. We can become fully developed, perfectly equipped, with no deficiencies.

Life's experiences test our faith. They also give some of the answers. I remember several years ago visiting a deacon in the hospital. He had just sustained a heart attack and was contemplating the long days of recovery ahead.

We talked over my sermon from the previous Sunday. In it I had told about a doctor who was asked by an anxious patient, "How long do I have to lie here?" The physician wisely replied, "Just one day at a time."

We all need this reminder. Jesus said, "Take no thought for the morrow." Don't borrow trouble. Don't fret and worry about the future. Take life one day at a time. As you do, you reach toward the maturity of a tested faith.

## Results in Joy

How do you react when trials come? We all have faced or will face sickness, sadness, death, despair, disappointment. How do these experiences affect you?

Different reactions are possible. The stoic sits and accepts life's calamities unmoved. "I can take it," he says.

The cynic shrugs with a sneer. "What's the use of trying anyway?"

The Muslim says "Kismet—it is fate!" as the irrevocable overtakes him.

But the Christian can cry, "God be praised!" Whatever happens in life cannot be so bad, but that God can bring good from it. Never forget: "And we know that all things work together for good to them that love God, to them who are the called according to his purpose" (Romans 8:28 KJV).

James says, "Consider it all joy, my brethren, when you encounter various trials" (1:2 NAS). With a play on words, he twice emphasizes the believer's unquenchable joy in the opening verses of this short letter. Let *joy* characterize your outlook. Count it as full or supreme *joy* when your faith is tested. Why? Because God can use it for good.

In verse 12 he explains, "Blessed is a man who perseveres under trial; for once he has been approved, he will receive the crown of life, which the Lord has promised to those who love Him." No wonder we can have joy. Look what's ahead!

Can you really view things this way? When misfortune comes, when tragedy strikes, when you get all the bad breaks, what will you do?

I'm not talking about shallow or superficial optimism. Someone told Bob Hope to let a smile be his umbrella. He said, "I tried that and got a mouthful of water!" It may seem that way.

But if you have Jesus by your side, it will make all the difference in the world. I know. My wife and I have gone through some difficult hours as a result of an auto accident in which we were involved eight years ago. We are reminded daily of some of the results. Gwen and I have often remarked that we do not see how those who have no Christian faith can take some of the things that life brings. But with Jesus, you can.

And *you* can have Him in your life, too. You must open your heart to let Him become king. You must do what He has asked, as the Scripture reveals. You must yield your life to follow Him without question, even when you can't see the way. When you do, you won't regret it.

His great invitation still stands:

Come unto me, all ye that labour and are heavy laden, and I will give you rest. Take my yoke upon you, and learn of me; for I am meek and lowly in heart: and ye shall find rest unto your souls. For my yoke is easy, and my burden is light (Matthew 11:28-30 KJV).

The Weaver
My life is but a weaving
   Between my Lord and me,
I cannot choose the colors
   He worketh steadily.

Ofttimes He weaveth sorrow,
   And I in foolish pride
Forget He sees the upper
   And I, the underside.

Not till the loom is silent
   And shuttles cease to fly
Shall God unroll the canvas
   And explain the reason why

The dark threads are as needful
   In the Weaver's skillful hand
As the thread of gold and silver
   In the pattern He has planned.

## Grounded Faith for Growing Christians

Now that you've read this chapter, try these Scripture passages: James 1, Romans 12:1, 2.

# 12

# GROWING CLOSER TOGETHER

Bud Wilkinson, the great football coach of Oklahoma University, once declared, "Before a team can play well, I believe that there has to be a feeling of importance attached to the activity that transcends the activity itself."

Priorities are all important. In Romans 12 Paul issues a clarion call for Christians to grow closer together. This theme needs to be echoed in our world.

We need it in the family. It has gotten so bad in one household, before Dad leaves to go bowling, and Mom, to her card party, they just tell their boy, "Son, we left a belt on the bed. If you do something wrong, hit yourself six times."

We need togetherness in the church also. Mary Lee Savermann defined "ecumenicism" as getting to know the opposite sects. We need that but, moreover, we need a real unity within the local assembly. We need to grow closer together just like the Christians of Rome.

Paul told them three ways to do this:

## Love One Another

Don't just pretend that you love others: really love them. Hate what is wrong. Stand on the side of the good. Love each other with brotherly affection and take delight in honoring each other (Romans 12: 9, 10 LB).

Genuine love can't be faked. You have to feel it in your heart. You have to mean it. The Christian must not bear himself "Like Judas to Christ, or Joab to Abner: a kiss and a stab" (Johnson).

You must have this kind of love for your husband or wife. After all, you're going to have to put up with a lot in a lifetime. Just the other day I said to my wife, "Gwen, will you still love me when I'm old and mean and grumpy?"

She replied, "Sure I do."

In addition to a general love for all, the Bible also stresses a particular love for the brethren (note Romans 12:10). Peter commands "Honor all men; love the brotherhood" (1 Peter 2:17 RSV).

William Barclay caught this meaning when he wrote:

We must love each other, because we are members of one family. We are not strangers to each other within the Christian church; much less are we isolated units; we are brothers and sisters of each other, because we have the one father, even God. The Christian church is not a collection of acquaintances; it is not even a gathering of friends; it is a family in God" (*Daily Study Bible–Romans*, p. 177).

Do you feel that kind of concern for others? Do you have this sort of love for your brethren in the local church? Do you show them that you care? Love one another!

Think first of your brother. That's the way to grow closer together. Paul said elsewhere,

Do nothing from selfishness or empty conceit, but with humility of mind let each of you regard one another as more important than himself; do not merely look out for your own personal interests, but also for the interests of others" (Philippians 2:3, 4 NAS).

## Help One Another

The next group of suggestions which the apostle gives in Romans 12 may be titled "help one another."

Never be lazy in your work but serve the Lord enthusiastically. Be glad for all God is planning for you. Be patient in trouble, and prayerful always. When God's children are in need, you be the one to help them out. And get into the habit of inviting guests home for dinner or, if they need lodging, for the night. If someone mistreats you because you are a Christian, don't curse him; pray that God will bless him. When others are happy, be happy with them. If they are sad, share their sorrow. Work happily together. Don't try to act big. Don't try to get into the good graces of important people, but enjoy the company of ordinary folks. And don't think you know it all! (v. 11-16 LB).

Too many are like the chap down in the deep South who saw a fellow start to leap from a building to his death. "Wait," he called up, "think of your mother!"

"I don't have a mother," the would-be suicide said hopelessly.

"Well, then think of your father," he pleaded the passer-by.

"My father is dead."

"But think of your wife."

"I never married."

"Well then, think of Robert E. Lee!"

"Robert E. Lee? Who's he?"

"Never mind, Yankee. Go ahead and jump!"

So often we shove others on toward a hopeless fate simply because we don't love them enough to help them. We don't care enough about them to demonstrate Christian concern.

We must always pray for one another. As we do this, it will lead to genuine interest and benevolence. When Christians lead the way in caring for the widows and orphans, government agencies will go by the board. The world will see the kind of love of which John spoke.

We know love by this, that He laid down His life for us; and we ought to lay down our lives for the brethren. But whoever has the world's goods, and beholds his brother in need and closes his heart against him, how does the love of God abide in him? Little children, let us not love with word or with tongue, but in deed and truth (1 John 3:16-18 NAS).

Julia Ward Howe asked a U.S. Senator once to help liberate a black man from a desperate situation. The legislator exclaimed, "Madam, I'm so busy with plans for the benefit of the whole race that I have no time to help individuals!"

Incensed by his lack of compassion, Mrs. Howe replied, "I'm glad our Lord never displayed such a calloused attitude!"

Jesus is our example in helping others. "Jesus," the Bible says, "went about doing good." So often we are simply content to go about! Do you want to grow closer to your brethren? Help them. Help one another.

Show hospitality to them. The Hebrew writer put it beautifully when he said, "Do not neglect to show hospitality to strangers, for by this some have entertained angels without knowing it" (13:2 NAS). This kind of opening of our home to guests is all too infrequent in our mechanized society. We expect computerized reservations, not Christians, to find us a hotel room. Many believers never open their home to a visiting missionary, evangelist, or Bible college choir member. They miss the blessing that comes to those who obey this Biblical command.

One of the simplest ways to help another is also one of the most neglected: "rejoice with those who rejoice, and weep with those who weep" (Romans 12:15). The ancient scholar Chrysostom explains, "One might think it was no difficult task to rejoice with others. But it is harder than to weep with them. . . . There is need of grace, however, to enable us, not merely to abstain from envying, but even with all our hearts to rejoice at the good fortune of a friend."

Try that—the next time your best friend gets a date with the gal you've been interested in! Try it—the next time your co-worker gets a promotion and a raise while you just get a nod from the boss! Try it—whenever you see a brother with a new car or new appliance or new house or whatever it is that you've been wanting, but can't get. This is a way we can share as brethren—and by it we can help one another.

To help one another requires that we have a proper estimate of ourselves. Humility does not mean that we think little of ourselves—simply that we don't think of ourselves. In this spirit, we can grow closer together. Finally, Paul suggests:

## Forgive One Another

"Never pay back evil for evil. Do things in such a way that everyone can see you are honest clear through. Don't quarrel with anyone. Be at peace with everyone, just as much as possible" (Romans 12:17, 18 LB).

This is not easy to do. But what good advice! If men can see we're honest; if men can see we avoid arguments; if men can see that we really try to be peacemakers—what a testimony our lives can have for the Prince of peace.

In words echoing the Sermon on the Mount, Paul points us to the higher plane of discipleship. Lee Carter Maynard observed, "Evil for evil is man's way. Evil for good is the devil's way. Good for evil is the Lord's way, and His way should be our way."

Hear the final words of the chapter:

Beloved, never avenge yourselves, but leave it to the wrath of God; for it is written, 'Vengeance is mine, I will repay, says the Lord. No, 'if your enemy is hungry, feed him; if he is thirsty, give him drink; for by so doing you will heap burning coals upon his head.' Do not be overcome by evil, but overcome evil with good (Romans 12:19-21 RSV).

What does that mean to you? Let me tell you what it meant to Corrie Ten Boom.

Imprisoned at the infamous Ravensbruck concentration camp, she had undergone cruel mistreatment by the Nazis. She saw her sister die there. After the war she spoke in a Munich church of God's forgiveness. When she concluded, to her horror, she saw one of her former guards approaching. She told of it like this:

'A fine message, fraulein! How good it is to know that, as you say, all our sins are at the bottom of the sea!'

And I, who had spoken so glibly of forgiveness, fumbled in my pocketbook rather than take that hand. He would not remember me, of course—how could he remember one prisoner among those thousands of women?

But I remembered him and the leather crop swinging from his belt. It was the first time since my release that I had been face to face with one of my captors and my blood seemed to freeze.

'You mentioned Ravensbruck in your talk,' he was saying. 'I was a guard in there.' No he did not remember me.

'But since that time,' he went on, 'I have become a Christian. I know that God has forgiven me for the cruel things I did there, but I would like to hear it from your lips as well. Fraulein—' again the hand came out—'will you forgive me?'

And I stood there—I whose sins had every day to be forgiven—and could not. Betsie had died in that place —could he erase her slow terrible death simply for the asking?

It could not have been many seconds that he stood there, hand held out, but to me it seemed hours as I wrestled with the most difficult thing I ever had to do.

For I had to do it—I knew that. The message that God forgives has a prior condition: that we forgive those who have injured us. 'If you do not forgive men their trespasses,' Jesus says, 'neither will your Father in heaven forgive your trespasses.'

I knew it not only as a commandment of God, but as a daily experience. Since the end of the war I had had a home in Holland for victims of Nazi brutality. Those who were able to forgive their former enemies were able also to return to the outside world and rebuild their lives, no matter what the physical scars. Those who nursed their bitterness remained invalids. It was a simple and as horrible as that.

And still I stood there with the coldness clutching my heart. But forgiveness is not an emotion—I knew that too. Forgiveness is an act of the will, and the will can function regardless of the temperature of the heart. 'Jesus, help me!' I prayed silently. 'I can lift my hand. I can do that much. You supply the feeling.'

And so woodenly, mechanically, I thrust my hand into the one stretched out to me. And as I did, an incredible thing took place. The current started in my shoulder, raced down my arm, sprang into our joined hands. And then this healing warmth seemed to flood my whole being, bringing tears to my eyes.

'I forgive you, brother!' I cried. 'With all my heart.'

For a long moment we grasped each other's hands, the former guard and the former prisoner. I had never known God's love so intensely as I did then.

If we want to grow closer together, we must love one another, help one another, and forgive one another. Will you do it? Will you do it at home? In the church: at school? Will you do it at work this week?

Jesus will help you. Turn to Him for strength.

## Grounded Faith for Growing Christians

Now that you've read this chapter, try these Scripture passages: Romans 12, 1 Corinthians 12.

# 13

# LIGHTS
# FOR
# A DARK WORLD

When Christ stood on the mount and preached His most famous sermon, He declared, "You are the light of the world" (Matthew 5:14 NAS). To whom were those words addressed? To statesmen, scholars, the socially prominent? You know the answer.

Plain, provincial people were His first followers. "Not many wise according to the flesh, not many mighty, not many noble" made up that band (1 Corinthians 1:26). But these people had something special. They had the Savior. What they had, they shared. Like them, the church today must assume the role of lights in a dark world.

## Relation

Jesus used many figures of speech to describe His personality and work to His followers. He called himself Bread, Shepherd, Door, Water, etc. One of the few terms with which He described both himself and His disciples was light.

The same Lord who stated "I am the light of the world"

shared that description with His brethren: "You are the light of the world." This indicates our relation to Him.

He is light in himself. He is the sun of righteousness risen with healing in His wings. He is the light that lights every man coming into the world. We shine only as we are touched and transformed by Him.

As Barclay put it, "The light with which the man of God shines is a borrowed light." God does not expect us to produce our own light, but to reflect that of Christ. We have Him within. Just as a bride may be aglow with the love for her husband, so the Christian must shine in spirit and deed as an expression of his love for the Master.

As lights, our relationship is also with others. We are kin to all "whose souls are lighted with wisdom from on high." We are placed in the world to show men the light of Christ.

When Robert Louis Stevenson was about six years old, he was sitting quietly by his window for a long time one evening. Fascinated, he watched the lamplighter making his evening rounds. His nurse came in to check on him. "What are you doing?" she asked.

"Watching a man make holes in the darkness," was his reply.

This is the Christian's task—to be a light in a dark world. Men who are depressed and discouraged need the light of Christian hope; men who are fallen and have failed need the light of Christian encouragement; men who question and worry need the light of Christian assurance. As we bring this light to them, we demonstrate our relation to the one who is the light of the world.

## Reason

"You are the light of the world. A city set on a hill cannot be hidden" (Matthew 5:14 NAS). Perhaps Jesus pointed to nearby city of Safed. Located boldly on a mountain peak, not far to the northwest of the Sea of Galilee, it was visible to the countryside. It was well protected and offered hope and security in wartime.

In a similar way, the Master tells us, believers are to stand as beacon lights to mankind. Those lost in sin, those troubled and discouraged—they need to see in us a reflection of what God can do for them. "It is no secret, what God can do; What He's done for others, He'll do for you."

The Christian's witness must not be hid. Someone has said, "There can be no such things as secret discipleship. Either the secrecy destroys the discipleship or the discipleship destroys the secrecy."

In his penetrating and frank spiritual autobiography, *The Taste of New Wine,* Keith Miller describes vividly the reason why we must tell others about Christ:

> In my reaction against legalistic, verbal religious 'scalp gathering,' I had for years decided that I would *live* my faith instead of *talk* about it. Now, I saw how totally selfish this 'live the faith and not talk about it' idea is. It reminds me of a man in a dread disease ward marvelously meeting the doctor who had perfected a cure. The patient, as he was being (secretly) cured, walked back and forth in the same ward sort of flexing his muscles as he moved beds around and various helped the other patients to *die more comfortably.* His display of new wholeness only led the other patients to envy *him* . . . leaving their own deep illness unattended to. I saw that this patient had to somehow *introduce his dying fellows to the physician* so that they too could begin to be healed from their loneliness and incompleteness. I realized that I was this patient. This introduction to Christ, I saw, would take some *words* of direction or at least indication. (Waco, Texas: Word Books, 1965), p. 89.

This is it. If you are a Christian—if you know what it is to have a sense of belonging to God, of peace and forgiveness—if you have experienced this joy, tell someone else. Bring them with you to worship and study. Invite them. Phone them. Call on them. Go by and get them.

After all, where do you put a light? Jesus reminds us that it surely doesn't go under a basket. Instead we place it high on a stand to shed light to the whole room. This is what you and I must do—at work, in school and home associations, on a date, wherever we are. We must seek to "give light to all who are in the house."

It should be impossible to do otherwise. Imagine saying to a light bulb, "You are free to function normally, only don't shed any light." It can't be. Men threatened early Christians if they kept talking about Jesus. They replied. "We cannot stop speaking what we have seen and heard" (Acts 4:20 NAS).

We are lights. Being lights, we must shine. However small it may seem, we can do something. I read of an ocean liner which was involved in a serious storm. The whole crew worked desperately. One man fell and was injured. The captain ordered him to his room.

Depressed because he could not help, the sailor suddenly heard the dreaded cry, "Man overboard!" He went to the porthole. The rolling waters were dark. He held his light out the window. Those feeble rays enabled the other men on deck to see the drowning man and save him.

This is what Jesus wants us to do. While our individual efforts may not seem to count for much, they may bring great good because we offer them faithfully.

Let the lower lights be burning,
Send a gleam across the wave;
Some poor, fainting, struggling seaman,
You may rescue, you may save.

## Result

If we are the light of the world, two results are assured by our Lord; men may see our good works and they may also offer glory to God for them.

Since men will see our behavior, whatever it is, we are warned to "abstain from all appearance of evil." Our good works speak more loudly than our good words.

I have changed in my evaluation of what is most important in my ministry. When I graduated from Bible college, I presumed that my ability in preaching sermons would be the most influential factor in my work. No longer is this my view.

I preached at one church for nine years—and preached perhaps 900 sermons there. If I were to return and ask the people to name or outline some of my messages, I doubt that few members could even list ten. But every person there would be able to tell how I lived, the spirit I showed, and the impression my life made.

As Charles Allen put it, "The minister brings the greatest light by the life that he lives rather than the words he speaks." So it is with every Christian.

Paul told the Thessalonians, "You also became imitators of us and of the Lord, having received the word in much tribulation with the joy of the Holy Spirit" (1 Thessalonians 1:6 NAS). It's frightening to think of having someone imitate you.

But people do look at you and think, "That's what the Christian life is." They *do* say it. They *do* judge us by it.

They see what you do on Sunday. They watch how you spend your money. They notice your choice of entertainment. They observe how you dress, the jokes you tell, the music you hear—and all of this tells them something. Is this the picture you want the world to have of Jesus? Do men see your *good* works?

The other result is that they can offer glory to God for what He has done in you and through you and because of you. We must not stop reading this text too soon. Men are not simply to see our good deeds and pat us on the back. There is no place for personal pride and selfish ambition.

Life's purpose is to glorify God. This is the whole of man (see Ecclesiastes 12:14). Resolve that you're not going to worry about making a name for yourself, but rather to make the name of Jesus known to others. Let the world know where you stand. It will cost you something. Shining is not an easy thing, as Guy King points out. Every sort of light involves self-consumption, self-giving. This is true whether it be a candle, an oil lamp, an electric bulb—or a Christian. There can be no shining without burning. But it is rewarding.

Keith Miller also told about a small group which helped him and others in his struggle of discipleship. A young married man in the group admitted to them one night:

> You know, sixteen weeks ago I came out here to laugh at you, and to prove to Betty that whatever it was she had found I didn't need. But after I'd been here an hour, I knew that this was important. And after two hours I knew you had found what I'd been looking for all my life . . . in all the wrong places. I knew you had found the 'name of the game' . . . the meaning of life (*The Taste of New Wine,* p. 74.)

## Grounded Faith for Growing Christians

Now that you've read this chapter, try these Scripture passages: Matthew 5:13-16; Acts 8:4-6; Romans 1:14-17.

# 14

# LET'S GROW

You may have heard about the large, imposing woman who asked a schoolgirl, "And what do you plan to do my dear, when you are as big as I am?"

The girl responded, "Go on a diet."

Growth isn't always popular. It isn't alway desirable. And it surely isn't always sought. But the kind of growth we've been talking about certainly is desirable —Christian growth, church growth, our development into the kind of people God wants us to be.

There are no shortcuts to this kind of growth. Dr. Medford Jones put it like this:

"Legitimate church growth is the increase of the congregation in quality and numbers as the functioning body of Christ. It is 'the building up of the body of Christ: till we all attain unto the unity of faith, and the knowledge of the Son of God, unto a full grown man, unto the measure of the stature of the fullness of Christ' (Ephesians 4:12, 13). This is the healthy, natural, balanced growth of the body. A church growing in this kind of Biblical wholeness is its own greatest witness. It is its own greatest evangelist as each person within it contributes in his own place according to his ability. Faith, love and all the fruitage of the Spirit must abound for the healthy growth of the church.

An interesting problem exists in our desire to grow. The Hebrew writer explained after mentioning Melchizedek: "Concerning him we have much to say, and it is hard to explain, since you have become dull of hearing" (Hebrews 5:11 NAS).

He goes on to outline the situation:

"For though by this time you ought to be teachers, you have need again for some one to teach you the elementary principles of the oracles of God, and you have come to need milk and not solid food. For every one who partakes only of milk is not accustomed to the word of righteousness, for he is a babe. But solid food is for the mature, who because of practice have their senses trained to discern good and evil" (5:12-14).

William Barclay titles this passage "the Christian who refused to grow up." Unfortunately churches are filled with these creatures! On the contrary, the Scripture explains, God expects Christian growth.

## Expected

"By this time you ought to be teachers!" How long have you been a Christian? Surely you can at least explain the basic facts about your faith to others. A teacher doesn't necessarily have to stand before a group of fifty—but he surely needs to be able to sit down with one person and share Jesus with him.

A child was asked how he liked the church service. He said, "Well, the music was OK, but the commercial was too long." I expect he speaks for quite a few. We might understand and excuse this in a child, but what about in an adult? Must the mature Christian live on a diet of spiritual "baby food"? The Hebrew writer condemned those who wouldn't eat solid food but still demanded milk.

The tragic picture of a person whose mind has not

developed properly cannot help but haunt the normal individual. Here is a person well up in years but without the mental ability that normally accompanies that age.

Even more serious is the lack of spiritual growth in our lives. Think of yourself in spiritual terms for a moment. What is your spiritual age—how long has it been since you became a Christian? How much have you grown in that period of time?

Consider these areas of your life:

● **Bible knowledge.** Have you been reading it on a regular basis following a purposeful plan? Do you take advantage of opportunities for group discussion and teaching?

● **Witnessing.** Do you find it easier to share your faith with others? Do you do so regularly?

● **Giving.** How does your stewardship measure up? Are you giving the same amount proportionately that you were when you became a Christian—or have you grown? Do you stay faithful in sending gifts even when you can't come?

● **Prayer.** Are you on speaking terms with God? Do you know the blessing that comes when you make spare moments prayer moments?

● **Music.** Are you learning more hymns and gospel songs? Do you have religious music to listen to at home or in your car with records, tapes, or FM?

● **Participation at church.** How much more do you do now in the total church program? Do you have a job? Have you volunteered for one?

● **Helping others.** Jesus clearly asserted the importance of brotherly love in His description of the judgment (Matthew 25). Do you show it?

How much have you grown? When distant relatives visit nephews and nieces they haven't seen for some time, the children quickly tire of hearing, "My, we'll have to put a brick on that child's head to keep him from growing so fast!" What is normal in a healthy child is also normal for a spiritually sound Christian. Perhaps you could say, "It is more blessed to grow than to recede!"

A man found an unused railroad ticket he had purchased when he was a boy. He boarded the train and tried to use the child's ticket. The conductor denied his request. Taking the case to court, the man lost. The verdict was that the purchaser of the ticket and the railroad entered into a contract when the ticket was sold. It was a child's ticket and the man had outgrown the provisions.

We are expected to grow with our years. What we excuse in a child, we dislike in a man. Society expects us to grow—and so does God!

## Neglected

But the unfortunate fact is that many neglect their responsibility to grow. The Scripture suggests one cause: many are grown "dull of hearing." They're like the soldier who was ordered, "Take that horse and have him shod." He saluted and left.

Later the officer came upon the young private again. "Did you get that horse to the blacksmith, soldier?"

A look of horror swept over the boy's face. Did you say *shod*?"

Most of us fail to listen as well as we should. This is one of the reasons why note-taking can be helpful as you listen to a sermon or Bible lesson. You are more likely to remember if you see as well as hear. You are more likely to remember what is said if you are personally involved.

If you have to keep having someone tell you where to look in the Bible to show the plan of salvation, the order of the New Testament church, or the basics of Christian living, you have been neglecting something vital.

Buy a Christian book. Attend a Bible-school class. Go to a prayer group. Share in Wednesday night Bible study. Pick up a take-home paper. Subscribe to a Christian magazine. Find some meat, not milk, and sink your teeth into it!

Apathy toward the things of God not only hinders progress, but causes you to slip backward. Christianity has been compared to riding a bicycle. You must keep going forward or you're liable to fall.

Growth is neglected in both knowledge and behavior. J. B. Phillips once remarked, "It is one of the curious phenomena of modern times that it is considered perfectly respectable to be abysmally ignorant of the Christian Faith." He noted that men who would be deeply ashamed of having their ignorance exposed in matters of music, literature, or farming seem not in the least perturbed to be found ignorant of the New Testament. This shouldn't be.

On a very personal basis, I want to challenge you to grow in your stewardship. I don't know what you give to the Lord. He does though. Are you really giving him a fair share of your income—or does he just get your pocket change? Do you write out a check for your church gift as soon as you deposit your paycheck in the bank—or do you just give God what you happen to have that you can spare, much like you'd tip a waitress?

If you have not been tithing, I challenge you to begin. You should whether you're an adult, a young person, a college student, retired, or whatever your place in live. Nine-tenths plus God's blessing will equal more. You'll find when you put God first that He'll provide for your needs (Matthew 6:33).

## Perfected

Isn't it time that we started making a consistent effort to develop and mature as Christians? If we ought to be teachers, as the Bible says, let's start doing it. Teach a Bible-school class. Sponsor a youth group. Help with children's church. Serve in the nursery. Call on others. "You can't teach what you don't know, and you can't lead where you won't go." Make this the time that you start perfecting your faith as Jesus commands.

Remember your spiritual age. See how much—or how little—you've grown. Set some goals. Then start to reach them.

Dr. Bonar once remarked that he could tell when a Christian was growing. "In proportion to his growth in grace, he will elevate his master. He will talk less of what he is doing, and become smaller and smaller in his own esteem, until, like the morning star, he fades away before the rising sun."

John the Baptist said of Jesus, "He must increase; I must decrease." This is the Christian's aim. By practice, our senses can be trained to discern good and evil. We can set our sights on higher goals.

Let's grow then. Let us see the ripened harvest fields of a needy world. I'm concerned about you as a person. God is, too. He wants you to grow. As the popular song says to Jesus, "to love thee more dearly, see thee more clearly, follow thee more nearly, day by day."

How about it?

Let's grow!

## Grounded Faith for Growing Christians

Now that you've read this chapter, try these Scripture passages: 2 Timothy 1:6-10; 2:1-7.